PRAISE FOR *IN THE LONG RUN*

Every time I meet Sundeep, I find myself asking the same question—"What's next?"—because he's always up to something meaningful. Whether it's his passion for sustainability, his commitment to running, or his ability to turn reflection into action, there's a quiet drive that defines him. In *In the Long Run*, he channels that same energy into a story of purpose and perseverance. True to form, Sundeep doesn't just talk about transformation—he lives it, and this book is a testament to that spirit.

AJAY VIJ
(Senior Country Managing Director, Accenture)

In The Long Run is a master class in personal evolution. It captures the grit behind growth and the discipline it demands, delivered in a voice that is both relatable and razor-sharp. What stands out is that the book doesn't just inspire, it enables. The frameworks are practical, grounded, and designed to move readers from self-awareness to meaningful action. This isn't just a personal story; it's a structured blueprint for transformation, meeting you where you are, and propelling you forward.

AMIT KUMAR
(Managing Partner & Global Head of Consulting, Wipro)

In The Long Run is not just a book about running. It is a reflection on life's deeper struggles and triumphs. Through his immersive storytelling, Sundeep lays bare the mental battles we all fight. With raw honesty and quiet humor, he shows how long-distance running became his crucible for resilience and reinvention. This book is a compelling reminder that the toughest battles are the ones we fight within, and that's exactly where transformation begins.

GANESAN RAMACHANDRAN
(Managing Director, Accenture)

My friend Sundeep has always believed that ordinary moments can hold extraordinary meaning, and he's proved it yet again with his second book *In the Long Run*. I was there with him when he set out to run 100 half marathons in 100 days, and again when he crossed that final finish line. What I saw was not just endurance, but joy, purpose, and an unshakable belief in the power of showing up. This book brings that journey to life. Insightful, honest, and full of heart—just like the man himself—this book is a must read for one and all.

PRASHANT SANGHVI
(Managing Director, Accenture)

Sundeep Singh's *In The Long Run* is a deeply introspective and remarkably candid narrative that captures the essence of personal transformation through the lens of long-distance running. With his trademark humility and honesty, Sundeep brings to life the internal tug-of-war between logic and instinct, comfort and courage, stagnation and growth. As someone who's watched Sundeep's journey unfold over the years, I found this book both inspiring and grounding. It's a must-read for anyone navigating their own pursuit of excellence — whether on the track, at work, or in life.

RAGHU POLISETTY
(Senior Managing Director, Accenture)

As a runner and a corporate leader, I found *In The Long Run* both relatable and deeply resonant. Sundeep beautifully captures the unspoken truths every runner knows: the silent negotiations with pain, the mental calculus of quitting versus continuing, and the quiet triumph of showing up, day after day. But this book goes far beyond running. His reflections on running mirror the struggles we face in life and leadership. This book is about the human spirit, about the courage to choose growth over comfort and purpose over habit. It's a quiet powerhouse of insight—raw, honest, and inspiring. Whether you're chasing a finish line or just trying to become a better version of yourself, *In The Long Run* is a reminder that the journey matters far more than the destination and that the real race is always within.

RASHMI MOHANTY
(Finance Professional and Ultramarathoner)

In The Long Run is not just a story about running; it is a powerful exploration of the inner conflicts that define us all. Through Sundeep's vivid story-telling, we see the tension between ambition and vulnerability. His extraordinary feat of running 100 half marathons in 100 days is a powerful testament to resilience and self-mastery. Beyond inspiring reflection, this book offers thoughtful frameworks that empower readers to shape their own paths of transformation. It is a must-read for all. It's a book only he could have written, and one that will inspire many to keep moving forward, one step at a time.

SANJAY DAWAR
(Lead Partner for One Consulting, PwC)

When it's about someone who hangs the moon the way Sundeep does, you know something special will follow. Watching Sundeep turn discipline into joy and ideas into action has always been inspiring. In *In the Long Run*, he opens a window into that mindset—the way he finds meaning in motion and balance in the chaos of modern life. It's a book that reminds you what quiet conviction can achieve. I strongly recommend reading it; you'll walk away reflecting on your own journey in a whole new way.

SCOTT PHARR
(Senior Managing Director, Accenture)

In The Long Run is a rare blend of narrative and insight, a deeply personal journey that doubles as a practical framework for self-mastery. Sundeep approaches long-distance running not as just a sport but as a metaphor for life's inner conflicts. His reflections are honest, sharp, and often surprisingly relatable. As a seasoned consulting professional, I saw in this book a blueprint for transformation, grounded not in theory, but in lived experience. It's the kind of book that stays with you long after the last page.

SURESH NANDURU
(Managing Director, Accenture)

Sundeep, whom I now know for over 15 years, is one unique professional who has evolved the most—from an exceptionally high-performing strategy management consultant to the foremost sustainability and circular economy leader, a serial marathon runner, and now a second-time author. He has done all of it over the last decade or so. Read his book to unleash new growth vectors in your life!

VISHVESH PRABHAKAR
(Sundeep's former colleague at Accenture)

IN THE LONG RUN

2427

IN THE LONG RUN

Lessons on Resilience, Focus, and Finding Yourself Beyond Work

SUNDEEP SINGH

JAICO PUBLISHING HOUSE

Ahmedabad Bangalore Chennai
Delhi Hyderabad Kolkata Mumbai

Published by Jaico Publishing House
A-2 Jash Chambers, 7-A Sir Phirozshah Mehta Road
Fort, Mumbai - 400 001
jaicopub@jaicobooks.com
www.jaicobooks.com

IN THE LONG RUN
ISBN 978-93-49358-60-7

First Jaico Impression: 2026

Printed by
Parksons Graphics Pvt. Ltd., Mumbai

CONTENTS

THE SPIRIT OF LONG-DISTANCE RUNNING TRIUMPHS

NOTE FROM THE AUTHOR

DURING my school days, I was a keen student—curious, reflective, and eager to learn—enjoying the process of learning more than the learning itself. The school environment, with my teachers and fellow students, was my happy space. It was no surprise that when I wrote my first book years later (*Chasing the Horizon*), the story was framed against the backdrop of an academic setup. It was written from the perspective of a 16-year-old aspirant to the Indian Institute of Technology (IIT), struggling to cope with academic pressures. The innocence and ambition of a young student underpinned the story.

But this one?

Well, this one wasn't a story I set out to live or narrate. It began as an unplanned chapter in life, one I could never have envisaged as a kid who preferred calculus over cricket. But life has a way of surprising you. One fine day, life introduced me to the world of running, apparently without any purpose or logic, and certainly without my permission. For the first time in my life, I had a hobby.

Over time, running became a canvas for reflection and a space in which to confront myself. It reignited the zeal for learning, something I had in abundance as a kid but had lost as I outgrew the academic phase of my life. I was ready to learn all over again, not the concepts of algebra or calculus this time, but life's deeper questions. I was ready to learn all over again, not from books or classrooms, but from moments that shake the ego and stretch the spirit.

It's not that the lessons dawned on me dramatically one fine day. They revealed themselves slowly, sometimes painfully, as I ran through the lonely stretches, where the only voice I could hear was my own.

This book is a collection of lessons, each acquired from the quiet clarity that emerges when you're too tired to pretend, lessons that are painful but life-changing, lessons that no one taught me at IIT or the Indian Institute of Management (IIM).

In this book, I've tried to package these lessons as guiding principles and frameworks that are relevant not just to running but to life. The best way to read this book is with your own story in mind. Whether you're recovering from a setback, striving toward a distant dream, or simply trying to hold yourself together, my hope is that these lessons meet you where you are, and help you move forward, with a little more clarity and strength.

Sundeep Singh

FOREWORD

SOME books are written with ink. This one was written with sweat, grit, and quiet resilience, word by word, kilometer by kilometer.

I've had the privilege of witnessing this story unfold up close. As Sundeep's wife and partner through life's highs and lows, I've seen every version of him—extremist, passionate, hopeful, frustrated, driven, defeated, and triumphant. But if there's one thing that has remained constant through the many chapters of his transformation, it is his willingness to keep moving forward, no matter what.

This book isn't just about running. It is about choosing to show up when it is easier not to. About leaning into pain when comfort is just a decision away. About listening to the quiet voice within when the world outside gets too loud. About having the courage to step out of one's comfort zone, not once, not twice, but every day.

When Sundeep first started running, I honestly didn't think much of it. Somewhere in my heart, though, I knew he would aspire to do things no one had ever done in this space. As my subconscious mind had anticipated, the hobby quickly became something else—his anchor, his mirror, his space for self-discovery. And as I watched him evolve through countless early mornings, torn muscles, injuries, finish lines, and quiet failures, I realized something important: The run was never about the road beneath his feet. It was about the road within.

Every chapter in this book has been lived, not just written. I've seen the toll it took. I've seen the discipline, doubts, planning, execution, and then planning again, the celebrations and the tears. I've also seen the wiser man emerge: one who isn't afraid to be vulnerable, to pause, to ask for help, to restart and give all he has, all over again.

To the reader picking up this book, I hope you find in these pages a little nudge in your own journey, whether that's lacing up your shoes, starting something new, or simply showing up for yourself. Because if there's one thing that I've learned from Sundeep, it's this: We are all stronger than we think. Sometimes, we just need to keep moving to find out.

With love and admiration,
Japneet

DOWN AND OUT

(January 15, 2023)

"Life is what happens to you while you're busy making other plans."

—John Lennon

1

NOT EVERY SETBACK IS THE END

The Battered Warrior

January 15, 2023

AS I boarded the flight to Mumbai, I felt a spring in my step. I was all pumped up to do well at the Tata Mumbai Marathon (TMM) 2023. And why not? I was at the peak of my running journey. I had recently qualified for the Boston Marathon, often regarded as the most coveted amateur long-distance running event in the world.

About half an hour into the flight, the air hostess arrived with refreshments. I politely declined. I wasn't about to let airline food derail my race prep. Instead, I pulled out my prepacked meal: fruit salad, pasta, and *idlis*—in that exact order, consumed with the care of a surgeon and the intensity of a man who treats pre-race carbs like chess moves, where every bite had to be perfectly timed. The man sitting next to me looked concerned, or possibly, alarmed. I could see him thinking, "Is he eating for two?" But it was all part of the pre-race day diet plan.

I reached the hotel reception around noon.

"Good afternoon, Sir. I guess you are here to run at the TMM," said the lady at the reception.

"Yes, I am. But how did you know that?" I asked, somewhat surprised.

"It's that time of the year. We see a lot of outstation runner guests on the TMM weekend," she said. "You look like a long-distance runner anyway, so it was easy," she continued. She was clearly the talkative type.

I smiled, nodding my head in affirmation.

As she carried out the check-in formalities, she spoke again, "Have you been running for a while?"

"Yes, for almost 10 years now. I recently qualified for the Boston Marathon. This is my last official event before I run at Boston in April this year." I wasn't missing the opportunity to brag about my Boston qualification.

"Wow! That's huge. Congratulations! All the best for the run tomorrow and the Boston Marathon," she said, handing the room keys to me.

By about 1 p.m., I was comfortably settled in my room. It offered a luxurious view of Mumbai's famous Sea Link. Beside the sea was a beautiful segment of the race route, which was all set to host over 50,000 runners the following day. After wandering in the room for a while, I sank down on the comfortable sofa, staring at nothing in particular through the expansive glass window. A few moments later, I got up, casually jogged on the spot to loosen the body, did a few stretches, and sank back into the sofa again. I was not sure why I did that. It was probably the adrenaline rush ahead of the race day.

At around 5 p.m., I started preparing my running gear. I carefully placed my T-shirt on the bed. It was a simple piece of cloth, but I handled it like a fragile piece of crystal. Next, I attached my running bib to the T-shirt, perfectly centered, scrutinized as carefully as an engineering drawing. I neatly arranged my running shorts, energy gels, banana, small water bottle, and running watch across the bed. My running shoes were placed just beside the bed. I took a step back and happily looked at my gear. It presented a vibrant and colorful picture. I did a quick mental check to ensure I wasn't missing anything.

T-shirt: Check

Shorts: Check

Shoes: Check

Head gear: Check

Socks: Check

Watch: Check

Hydration: Check

Energy gels: Check

I went on with a few more items to be sure that everything was ready. It all looked spotless. I felt ready. I was ready. I was all set to ace the race.

Nothing could go wrong.

Until 3:30 a.m.

The moment the alarm went off, I leaped out of bed.

"It's show-time!" I whispered excitedly.

Just as I took my first step, I felt a sharp pain in my lower back, a momentary sensation that came and disappeared in a flash. I froze instantly, wondering where the hell that sensation had come from. I'd never felt it before.

A few moments later, I took a tentative step.

Big mistake.

The pain returned, angrier now, like a warning I had dared to walk past. I froze. My body refused to move. I was stuck, standing in the dark, halfway between being ready for glory and being ready for the emergency room.

I needed to call someone for help. But my phone—and with it, any hope of calling for help—was lying across the room. My physical state made it impossible for me to get to it.

I stood there for several minutes, frozen, clueless about what to do next. Something had to give, for I couldn't stand there forever. Overcoming agonizing pain, I lowered myself to go down on my knees and palms. The new position was equally painful, but somewhat better than the previous one. I was now supporting myself on four contact points, like a man reenacting a wildlife documentary.

"So much for the full marathon I had come to run," I haplessly thought to myself.

I made several attempts to move, but every effort triggered unbearable pain. I even wondered whether this harrowing experience was real or a nightmare that felt terribly real. I wanted to pinch myself to check whether I was awake. But that would have required me to take my palm off the ground, a luxury that my body refused to offer in that moment. I wondered what evil deeds I had done in life to be brought down on my knees like that.

I must have lain on the floor for an hour with that unbearable pain. After a while, I heard jubilant shrieks from a distance. I wondered whether I was hallucinating or the marathon had actually started. With what seemed like a gigantic effort, I crawled to one side of the room to look out of the glass window.

TMM 2023 had taken off. The runners were on the streets. My fellow runners.

And I? I was watching from the floor of my hotel room, teary-eyed and broken, in more ways than one.

I kept staring at them almost in disbelief. I was supposed to be there with them on the beautiful roads of Mumbai that morning. But destiny had other plans for me. A tear trickled down my cheek as I became aware of my loss. I wondered whether I would ever be able to run again. It all seemed over. I closed my eyes, thinking about the beautiful journey I had undertaken to reach that painful moment.

Tata Mumbai Marathon 2023 takes off as I helplessly watch from the confines of my hotel room.

IF YOU CAN RUN, I CAN TOO

(2014–2015)

"The miracle isn't that I finished. The miracle is that I had the courage to start."

—John Bingham

2

FOLLOW THE SIGNS; THEY KNOW THE WAY

Marathon? Sure, why not?

IT was another usual day at the office. You know the kind: caffeine-fueled, calendar-heavy, and already exhausting by 9:01 a.m. As I entered my cabin, I casually glanced at the calendar. It looked like a packed agenda: client meetings, a project review, a recruitment interview, a team huddle, and then a few more meetings. By the time I read through it, I was tired enough to consider a second life as a professional sleeper.

At around 11 a.m., a gentleman named Gautham Krishnan walked in for his final job interview. He looked bright and smart, bubbling with energy—everything I wasn't feeling that morning. His demeanor made me more conscious of my lethargy. I made a mental note not to yawn.

The interview began the usual way, a ritual exchange of uninspired questions and overly rehearsed answers: *"Tell me about yourself," "What is your biggest weakness?"*, *"Where do you see yourself in five years from now?"*, and so on. Gautham at least tried to spice up the conversation with some cheeky responses, but I guess it was a case of garbage in, garbage out. We both went on for a while with our garbage contributions before I inadvertently asked a question that would change my life.

"What do you do when you're not working?" I asked.

"I run half marathons and full marathons," he said, as though talking about a casual stroll in the park.

"A half marathon is 21.1 kilometers. A full marathon is 42.2 kilometers," he added matter-of-factly, as if these numbers weren't completely outrageous to the average person with a fondness for elevators.

I blinked. The longest distance I'd ever run was an 800-meter dash in school. And even then, I'd stopped before the finish line because my lungs filed a protest. This man was talking casually about doing 50 times of that distance, on the weekends, *for fun!* Was he trying to psyche me out? I wasn't sure, but I pulled in my tummy to appear leaner than I was.

The interview ended. He left. I moved on to my next meeting. But his words didn't leave me. I continued to think about that brief conversation, *"42.2 kilometers on the feet, for fun. Wow!"*

It stuck with me. Like a whisper. A sign. A nudge from the universe. The kind of nudge that gets ignored under Excel sheets and quarterly targets. But not this time. For some inexplicable reason, it felt like life was giving me a cue. It was not the first time I was feeling that way. But on similar occasions previously, my self-image of the logical IIT-IIM-consulting professional came in the way of my hearing those whispers. This time, though, I was prepared to give that inner voice a chance. I remembered the famous quote from Steve Jobs, "Have the courage to follow your heart and intuition. They somehow already know what you truly want to become. Everything else is secondary."

The universe always finds a way to nudge us toward where we're meant to be, but most of us are too busy to pay attention.

Later that night, I stepped out for a jog. It was probably my way of giving that inner voice a chance. Or maybe it was just a case of the competitor in me trying to check how far I could go. I was certain that even with an all-out effort, I wouldn't be able to go beyond 5 kilometers. I was disappointed to discover that I had grossly overestimated my physical ability. I managed a little less than 2 kilometers.

Ego bruised. Pride dented. Hamstrings outraged.

My dismal performance in that inconsequential late-night run did inflict some ego wounds. I kept brooding about it for several days, hoping that the feeling would fade. But that didn't happen. The more I thought about it, the more I wanted to do something about it. In the hope of resurrecting my crushed ego, I vowed to run a marathon soon. It was a rubbish target, rubbish because it was purely based on my petty ego and there was no serious thought put into it. I had no clue about what it would take a novice like me to run a marathon.

What followed was a bizarre mix of discipline and chaos. I ran every night, sometimes at midnight, after long workdays. But there was no method to this madness. All I did was run, run some more, and then run just a little more. Making time every day wasn't easy, certainly not with the unpredictability that consulting brings. But somewhere along the way, I learned something: There's no such thing as a lack of time. If something is a priority, you find time for it. And for me, running had quietly become a priority.

There is no such thing as a lack of time; there is only a lack of priority.

On most days, I would run a nice little loop within my society complex. The length of the loop was perfect, almost as if designed to make it easy to track distance. It measured exactly two-thirds of a kilometer. Three laps meant two kilometers. Simple math.

It didn't feel comfortable at first, but I soon started enjoying it. There is something supremely romantic about being all by yourself, beneath the moonlight, immersed in random thoughts, drenched in a sweaty T-shirt, putting one foot in front of other, enduring all the physical discomfort. The steady thumping of my feet on those dark late-night runs added to the special effects. Yes, I was beginning to fall in love with that feeling, a feeling that amalgamated joy and discomfort in the same moment. I'd always believed that there is a superhero in each of us. Those late-night runs helped me connect with my inner superhero.

I would see several regular walkers during my runs around the society loop. I did not know them personally. But when you see the same people at the same place doing the same thing day after day, you build a kind of unspoken bond with them. I started to connect with those people in a strange way, strange because it rarely entailed a conversation. With some people, it would be a hand wave; with others, a warm smile; and with still others, just a subtle nod to acknowledge their presence. For some inexplicable reason, I had started cherishing those mute connects too. I would look forward to those connects as much as the run itself.

"Why do you run so much?" "Don't you find it monotonous?" "What do you think about when you run?" If you are a runner, you have surely been asked these questions at some point. I was no exception. People had started asking me these questions, and I felt great about it. Not that I had any intelligent answers, but it felt good to know that people were perceiving me as a runner. On most occasions, I would just smile and make up some decent-sounding answer. Over time, I developed a mental repository of responses that I could draw from.

I would often reply, "It's my 'me' time," as if I were off to meditating in the Himalayas instead of huffing down dusty Gurugram roads.

I probably heard someone say it once and must have found it fancy. So, it became a part of my repository. But deep within, did I really know the answer? Well, no.

In my profession as a consultant, I've always had the license to respond with, "It depends." But in this case, it doesn't even depend. Take the classic question, "What do you think about when you run?", for instance.

Honestly?

Anything. Everything. Nothing.

On some days, I think about the weather. On other days, it's my bank balance. There have been mornings when I've thought about Newton's laws of motion or Sachin Tendulkar's farewell speech. On an unusual day, you could even catch me thinking how nice it would have been if the Titanic hadn't sunk. The point is I could be thinking of just about anything, with the exception of politics. The point also is that I am never thinking about anything that could put me on the path to a breakthrough discovery.

With such a wide spread of random and inconsequential thoughts, how is one supposed to answer this question? Sometimes, I also wonder if these thoughts are really random. Maybe they mean something. Maybe we runners just haven't evolved enough to connect the dots. But that's a topic for another day.

For now, let's get back to running.

It had been over six months of following my new routine, and I was beginning to feel the changes. I felt lighter. More alive. More deliberate about how I spent my time. I'd even started trimming wasted minutes during the day so I could make it to my evening runs on time. My waistline was also quietly receding, and I wasn't complaining about that.

The only thing that was probably not changing fast enough for me was my running ability itself. I was still stuck at around 14 or 15 kilometers. That wall just wouldn't budge.

It was late July. The monsoon was in full swing. I was navigating Gurugram's signature water-clogged roads when a massive billboard caught my attention.

A sprinter, mid-stride. Muscles flexed. Eyes focused.

The caption read:

"Airtel Delhi Half Marathon. India's biggest running carnival. Coming soon. Are you ready?"

Something stirred in me. The idea of becoming a half marathoner suddenly didn't feel so far-fetched. The adrenaline surged, and then reality followed.

I took a deep breath and read it again.

"Airtel Delhi Half Marathon. India's biggest running carnival. Coming soon. Are you ready?"

"Hell, no. I am not," I thought.

But then something inside me whispered, just like Gautham's casual bombshell in that interview months earlier, *"If he can run, I can too."*

I was still struggling to push past 15 kilometers. To become a half marathoner, I'd need to run 21.1 kilometers in three hours.

I checked the event details. The race was in November. I had four months.

"Should be enough," I thought, fist clenched in quiet optimism.

Later that night, I brought it up with Japneet—my sounding board for all important decisions.

"I have signed up for a half marathon on November 23."

"Fantastic!" she beamed. "Ekam and I will come cheer for you."

"It's a road race, not a loop on a track. You probably won't spot me. Also, I'll get self-conscious if I know you're watching," I grinned.

"Okay, then we will celebrate when you come back."

Brief pause.

"Honestly, right now, I'm less worried about the celebration and more about surviving the race. I haven't been able to get past 15 kilometers for the past three months."

"Why don't you consult a fitness trainer? They might be able to help."

"Do you know someone?"

"There's a gym nearby, Bomiso Gym. Give it a shot."

I was initially reluctant. The idea of asking someone for help never really appealed to me. Asking is for people who don't Google. It feels like the trait of a lackadaisical person who has no control. When I get lost while traveling, I would rather roam around directionless for a while than bother asking for directions. This is how I used to think back then. Of course, that thinking has changed over time and changed for good.

Asking for help doesn't mean you're failing; it just means you're serious about getting it right.

Run, rest, train ... repeat

A few days later, I walked into Bomiso Gym. It was bigger than any other gym that I'd been to. Within minutes, a strong, muscular, bespectacled gentleman approached me with a warm smile and a post-workout sheen. His physique resembled that of a weightlifter, though his demeanor was of a well-groomed corporate professional.

"Hi, my name is Anubhav. How can I help you?" he asked.

"Hello, Sir. My name is Sundeep. I am preparing for a running event and could use some guidance."

"Great. Let's find a spot and talk."

He courteously showed me inside the gym. I learned he was the gym owner—a former corporate professional who had left it all to pursue his passion for fitness.

"Anubhav, I am looking to run a half marathon in November. I've been training for the last six months, but despite my best efforts, I am unable to go beyond 15 kilometers."

"So, how do you train?" he asked.

"I run every day."

"And what else do you do?"

An awkward pause.

"Umm ... Nothing," I replied.

We both smiled.

Just two simple questions, and I already knew the answer. Sometimes, you need a sounding board to reflect the truth you're pretending not to see.

We spoke for nearly an hour, about diet, strength training, flexibility, hydration, and sleep. I realized how absurdly ignorant I had been. Ignorance, they say, is bliss, but terms and conditions apply. I had been training like a man in a stationary bus, sprinting with determination but going nowhere. I could have continued doing that for a lifetime, and my coordinates would still not have changed. It was a stationary bus, after all. But I had a few tools now to actually move the bus.

Later that night, I sat down with a notebook and a pen. We, the so-called strategy consultants, love doing that. The other thing we love is the power of three. We love to think in threes: three ideas, three big messages, three actions, three insights. When we talk to our clients, our pitch often goes like this: "This is where you are. This is where you need to be. And there are three things you need to do to get there."

So, I did what we do best. I identified three magical levers to bridge the gap between where I was and where I needed to be. I moved to a fresh page and neatly wrote: (i) Eat healthy and stay hydrated; (ii) Strength train twice a week; (iii) Sleep seven hours a night.

Simple on paper. Life-changing in practice.

I accepted the mantra that food is a source of fuel, not entertainment. There was a clear instruction to my mind that any food that helped with my running goals was good. With that acceptance, even foods like bitter gourd, beetroot, and sprouts started finding their way to my plate. My usual favorite foods—cookies, chips, aerated soft drinks—quietly disappeared. My taste buds were not too happy to begin with, but I was prepared to ignore them in pursuit of my running goals.

If you belong to a Punjabi family, it is not easy to sustain these eating habits. Besides fighting your own temptations, you have to deal with people around you. At times, some of them would nudge me to take just a little; sometimes, others would subtly sympathize that I had to put up with such food. The nastiest of them would socially ridicule me for my eating choices. Over the years, I've encountered all of these types. I've always wondered why they behave the way they do. I don't think they are worried about what I eat (why would they be, anyway?), but they find it difficult to accept that someone could resist the temptations that they could not.

Your detractors will always try to hold you back. You cannot stop them, but you can certainly ignore them.

Whatever be their reasons, my way of dealing with such detractors is quite simple. No discussion, no debate, no justifications. Just ignore them, and do what I have to do.

I revamped my training plan too. "Run, run, run" became "Run, rest, strength train, repeat." I added lunges, planks, squats, and burpees—workouts that could happen anywhere, anytime.

I stopped glorifying sleep deprivation. Earlier, I used to think waking up at 5 a.m. after sleeping late was a badge of honor. Now, I understood that recovery was as critical as effort. I stopped sacrificing sleep for self-image. It was probably still acceptable, but more as an exception than as a rule. As a simple guiding principle, I started striving for seven hours of quality sleep daily.

The human body is probably God's most fascinating creation. I would be lying if I claimed that I had started understanding it fully. But one thing I did realize is that if you provide it with the right stimulus, the body responds beautifully. Push it a little bit, fuel it with the right food, enrich it with the right thoughts, allow it to get ample rest, and you see transformative changes over time.

With these changes in place, my running began to shift. The wall started to move.

And by the time winter arrived, I was ready.

I was ready to embrace the carnival called Airtel Delhi Half Marathon (ADHM) 2014. I was ready to take my first fledgling steps, following the quiet signs life had planted along the way.

Whenever I speak at B-schools, there's one question that never fails to pop up: "How do you juggle consulting, running marathons, and writing books at the same time?"

I usually smile, pause, and resist the urge to say, "Caffeine and denial."

Instead, I talk about **F.O.C.U.S**, a framework that's less about doing more and more about doing what matters.

F.O.C.U.S: Five habits to make the most of your time

<table>
<tr><td>F: Frame your priorities</td><td>Be deliberate about what truly matters.</td><td>People who "find time" for everything aren't doing everything; they're just crystal clear about what matters most.
• They don't confuse busy with important.
• They don't suffer from fear of missing out (FOMO).
• They pick their battles.</td></tr>
<tr><td>O: Own your calendar</td><td>Treat your time as a valuable personal asset.</td><td>Smart people understand that everything you say "yes" to is a "no" to something else.
• They say "no" without guilt.
• They avoid multitasking.
• They declutter their schedule—no meetings without meaning.</td></tr>
<tr><td>C: Conserve your energy</td><td>Save your energy like a scarce resource—because it is.</td><td>Effective people pick their battles carefully because everything draws energy from your finite reserves.
• They don't overexert to prove they're productive.
• They protect their recovery through sleep, solitude, and breaks.
• They are deliberate about what they say "yes" to.</td></tr>
</table>

U: Unlearn distracting habits	Let go of default behaviors that drain time and attention.	People who value their time are often quietly watching over themselves. • They delete, mute, or block what doesn't merit attention. • They notice their default time drains and question them. This one always reminds me of what an old friend once said: "I used to think I had no time. Then, I tracked it. It turned out I had a PhD in scrolling."
S: Start small	Don't wait for the ideal moment.	Biases, in general, are bad, but bias for action is an exception. This is how high achievers are wired. • They don't wait for big launches. • They understand the best time to begin is often now. • They test, iterate, and build momentum with action.

Key Messages

i. **Stay alert to the gentle signals life offers along the way.**

Life rarely screams. It nudges—through chance conversations, roadside billboards, or casual remarks during job interviews (as was the case for me). It's a bit like a treasure hunt. Subtle cues or signs could steer us to the ultimate treasure in life: happiness. We can either stay trapped in our daily rut and miss these cues or take the plunge when life throws these cues our way.

ii. **Asking for help isn't a sign of weakness; it's a mark of those truly committed to their goals.**

Knowing the answer is good. But knowing how to find the answer? That's far more powerful. Don't fall for the myth of solitary brilliance. There is no glory in figuring it all out alone. Life is too short, and there are too many questions. Ask. Reach out. Borrow maps from fellow travelers. As they say, we are all a bunch of monkeys on an organic spacecraft hurtling through the universe. No one knows it all. So, I am glad that I asked Anubhav for his guidance at the right time.

iii. **There is no such thing as a lack of time to do the things that you truly want to do.**

An effective framework to make the most of your time is F.O.C.U.S: Frame your priorities; own your calendar; conserve your energy; unlearn distracting habits; and start small.

3

CRAWL IF YOU MUST, BUT KEEP MOVING

IWIK: You can't sprint 21K

AS race day drew closer, my mind became a bubbling cauldron of questions:

"How would I remember the route?"

"How will they track my running time?"

"Can we listen to music during the run?"

"Do we get disqualified if we walk along the way?"

"What happens if I need to take a bio break?"

"Do I need to carry a water bottle along the run?"

I called a few runner friends who had participated in running events. Based on their inputs, I stitched together a mental image. I imagined a handful of slightly crazy runners, guided by a few volunteers, taking over the streets of Delhi on a misty morning ...

... And then I arrived at the venue.

My mental image fell flat on its face.

It was a full-blown spectacle: bright lights, thumping music, Zumba warmups, hydration booths, portable toilets, security, media vans, and a sea of runners in neon gear. Some runners were stretching, some were speed-walking to the start line, and others were busy in elaborate pre-run rituals. The energy was infectious. It didn't feel like a run. It felt like Delhi was hosting a grand street festival in running shoes.

Was it really a running event? Sure, it was.

But it was much more. It was a carnival. A grand, chaotic, beautiful carnival.

As I waited anxiously at the start line, jogging nervously in place, memories came flooding in: late-night solo runs, awkward strength training in my bedroom, quiet conversations with Japneet. Before I could linger in nostalgia, the music swelled.

"TEN, NINE, EIGHT ..."

The crowd roared.

"SEVEN, SIX, FIVE ..."

My heart pounded.

"FOUR, THREE, TWO, ONE ... GO! Let's run, Delhi!"

"My first half marathon!" I whispered to myself.

Off I went like a bullet. That's the thing about first-timers—we let the adrenaline dictate our pacing strategy. I zipped past the others, confused why they weren't pushing harder.

"Maybe they didn't practice hard enough," I thought, my chest swelling with pride and strides opening a tad wider.

The run route entailed some of the most iconic spots in Delhi: Jawahar Lal Nehru Stadium, Lodhi Garden, India Gate, and Jantar Mantar, among several others. Add to that the vibrant music bands, the beats, the cheerful crowd, the super-active volunteers, and the hydration zones all along the route. It was an ambience I had never imagined or experienced before. I had never seen Delhi like this. It was stunning.

I thanked my stars again for that fateful interview with Gautham, who, unknowingly, had set this whole journey in motion.

I continued to push along as hard as I could, not realizing that I was going much faster than what I could sustain. By the seventh kilometer, the magic started to fade. The spring-like feeling under my feet suddenly started to wane. My shoulders started to drop. A couple of kilometers later, other runners started overtaking me. Some of them gently stared at me as they went past. They seemed to be answering the question I never asked: "This is not a sprint. You need to respect the distance, buddy."

How often do we make that mistake in life? Start with wild enthusiasm, throttle at full power, and burn out halfway? Whether it's the overzealous professional slogging through the early years only to crash into midlife exhaustion, or someone on a radical diet that collapses within a week, we often forget that the real game is longevity, not just intensity.

Life is a marathon, not a short-distance sprint. Longevity matters. Pace your journey accordingly.

So, I dragged along.

By the 15th kilometer, I considered quitting.

My legs were heavy. My breathing felt labored.

Then came the inner voice, the soft yet insistent whisper that shows up right when you're about to give up:

"Running is nothing more than a series of arguments between the part of your brain that wants to stop and the part that wants to keep going."

Those words surfaced, uninvited. And thank God they did. I continued to chug along.

By the 18th kilometer, I was done. Not metaphorically. Really done. I wanted to miraculously vanish from the track, evaporating into thin air so no one would notice I'd quit. The physical fatigue was brutal, but the mental battle was worse. I was negotiating with myself every second. I once again seriously considered bringing an end to my agony. The thought was supremely enticing.

Just when I was about to pull the plug, I saw a little boy holding a placard:

"You are almost there."

I was sinking, and the boy was extending a rope for me to latch onto. Something clicked inside.

I didn't speed up. I didn't get stronger either. But I kept moving. I continued to put one foot ahead of the other.

Left, right. Left, right. Repeat.

I eventually crossed the finish line.

In the months leading to that race, I had often visualized how I would react on crossing the finish line. I had always imagined leaping into the air with victorious fist pumping, maybe even a slow-motion moment like those on cheesy sports magazine covers.

What actually happened?

I looked like a vulnerable athlete performing a skeleton dance. Collapsing felt like a genuine possibility. I was feeling dead, physically and mentally. Yet, I was alive, probably more alive than I had ever been in my life.

And yes, I was an official half marathoner too.

I finished the run in 1 hour, 43 minutes, and 7 seconds.

A sight of misery and struggle at the end of my first half marathon (skeleton dance)

Registration window closed; sanity followed suit

By the time I got back home, my head was spinning. I was so exhausted that even ringing the doorbell felt like a full-body workout. I leaned against the wall and waited for Japneet to open the door.

"Congratulations!!" shouted Japneet as she excitedly opened the door.

"You nailed it," She continued as we both entered the house.

"That's my dad!" Ekam chimed in proudly.

They both took my hand and led me to the dining table. And there it was, a surprise celebration. A cake with one of my favorite training photos on it. The caption beneath it read, 'Congratulations, Dad!'

Japneet had gone all out with a table full of handpicked delicacies. She knew this was the moment to indulge. And she was right.

"So, how was the run?" asked Japneet.

"It was tough."

"It was a half marathon. Surely, it had to be."

"No, I mean I made it tougher than it needed to be."

"What do you mean?" she asked.

"I got carried away in the first few kilometers and ran too fast. That hurt me in the later stages. Toward the end, I seriously considered aborting the run."

"I am sure you would never do that."

Brief pause.

"But honestly, I came very close," I replied after a bit of deliberation.

"That's okay. It was your first race. You'll pace better next time."

I smiled, wondering if I was ever going to participate in another running event. The atmosphere was electrifying, but the pain I had to bear in the last few kilometers! Was it really worth going through that experience again? I wasn't sure.

Over the next few days, I kept revisiting the race day in my mind. I replayed every stretch of road, every mistake, every win. I thought about the training that led up to it. I was happy to have achieved what I had set out for myself. But there was also a strange, hollow feeling that I couldn't understand at first. I had done exactly what I set out to do. Then why did I have this lingering sense of letdown? Maybe it had something to do with the way I finished the run. Perhaps it was something more fundamental that I was unable to define.

After mulling it over, I realized what was bothering me.

It wasn't the race. It was the void that followed.

For months, my life had revolved around preparing for the ADHM. Now, suddenly, there was nothing to work toward. No goal. No calendar marker. I could already feel myself slipping—discipline loosening, late nights creeping back in, and mindless eating making a comeback. I didn't want to go back to the version of myself that I had left behind.

When there's nothing to aim for, it's easy to wander aimlessly. That's when bad habits sneak back in, not like intruders, but like old friends.

The only way out was clear: I needed another goal. I needed to sign up for another race to keep myself sane and happy.

A quick internet search pointed me to the Standard Chartered Mumbai Marathon (SCMM) in January 2015. But there was a catch: The half-marathon slots were sold out, and only full-marathon registrations were open.

My jaw dropped, and then tightened.

I thought for a few minutes.

What followed was a familiar civil war between the two voices in my head: the logical "me" that has the ability to reason and is sensible, and the defiant "ME" that loves new challenges and wants to do its own thing. Under normal circumstances, the two of them coexist in perfect harmony. But in moments of stress or dilemma, they often get polarized as two distinct voices trying to pull me in opposite directions.

me: *"You just missed it. Had you thought about it few days back, you could have registered for the half marathon."*

ME: *"So what? I will register for the full marathon."*

me: *"Don't be stupid. You are forgetting your plight in the last few kilometers of the ADHM. Can you imagine yourself going the whole distance all over again?"*

ME: *"No, I can't, not with my current level of fitness. But this event is still a month away. I will train for it."*

me: *"Are you out of your mind? One month won't be enough."*

ME: *"How do you know?"*

me (frustrated): *"Because it is not a regression line that you can conveniently extrapolate on graph paper. This is real distance, real sweat, real fatigue. Do you remember how long it took you to move from 15 to 21 kilometers? For heaven's sake, we are now talking about moving from 21 to 42 kilometers!'*

ME: *"Maybe you are right, but we will only know if you let me try. So, will you please shut up now?"*

I sometimes wonder what an exquisite, bizarre little creation of God the human mind is—a 1,400-gram powerhouse, with so much trapped in it. All our fears, aspirations, desires, logic neatly housed in a small, unfathomable box. A part of it wants to conform, and another part wants to rebel.

The logical "me" finally gave up.

And I signed up for my first full marathon.

The finish line that earned me a new title: Marathoner

The SCMM was just a month away. The fact that I had signed up to transition from a half to a full marathon in such a short time said less about my fitness and more about my ignorance.

I didn't truly understand what it takes to train for a full marathon. Or maybe I did, but I just preferred to live in denial since I had already clicked the *Register* button.

"It's just two back-to-back half marathons," I told myself. "I've done one. Now, I just need to do two. How hard could that be?"

The intellectual "me" knew it didn't work that way, certainly not in the world of long-distance running. But the rebellious "ME" wasn't one to let logic spoil a good challenge.

> *Sometimes, it's good to leap before you're ready and trust that you will figure it out midair.*

So, I got started.

Over the following weeks, I did plenty of long-distance runs. With each run, I progressively increased the distance, stretching the boundaries of my comfort zone one kilometer at a time. I touched 26. Then 28. Then 30. Then 32.

And one thing became painfully clear.

Yes, a full marathon is mathematically two half marathons in distance.

But in effort? It's entirely different.

Something mysterious happens when you enter the 30+ kilometer zone. At least, it did for me. Every time I reached that distance, it felt like I had entered some prohibited no-man's land with heavily restricted entry criteria. Like I'd wandered into a military base without permission. My body would protest. My mind would send alerts. My spirit would start negotiating. That zone was not meant for casual runners. Entry had to be earned, and I hadn't earned it yet. Every time I approached that distance, it felt like I had breached a sacrosanct law of the land, which necessitated immediate remedial action, requiring me to stop with immediate effect.

With less than a week to go, my longest training run was 32 kilometers. No matter what I tried, I couldn't push past it. Worse still, I had developed a distinct phobia for anything beyond that. Reaching 33 kilometers might as well have been on a different planet.

Race day: January 18, 2015

The buzz at the SCMM venue was electric. The atmosphere in Mumbai mirrored what I had experienced at Delhi's Jawaharlal Nehru Stadium a few months earlier, except this felt even bigger, deeper, like the city had embraced the event as its own.

I stood at the start line, both anxious and excited.

"If all goes well, I will be a marathoner in a few hours from now," I grinned to myself.

The run started.

I jogged along the beautiful roads of Mumbai, making a conscious effort not to think too far ahead. I focused instead on feeling the joy all around me. I keenly watched the runners bubbling with energy, as if they were on to something special.

Being on the streets of Mumbai felt surreal. It triggered a strange feeling of *déjà vu*. Maybe I had imbibed bits of the Mumbai spirit through Bollywood classics on the big screen. It felt like every Indian grows up with a mysterious relationship to Mumbai. Something made me feel that a part of me, however small, belonged to that beautiful city.

Strangely enough, the popular Bollywood classic, *"... Ye hai Mumbai meri jaan ..."* played in my mind as I joyfully jogged through those unexpectedly familiar streets. I couldn't recall when and where I had last heard that song. Yet, it was playing in my mind as if I chanted that song every day.

I jogged along.

Roughly two hours later, I hit the halfway mark: 21.1 kilometers. Still in familiar territory, I felt okay physically. I had trained for up to 32 kilometers, after all. I felt I had enough ammunition left to go the distance, but my mood had started to shift a bit. The euphoria had given way to sobriety. I was beginning to think about how far I had come and how much further I had to go.

My runner friends had always warned me to tread this middle part carefully, and I recalled their wise advice:

"By this time, the start line is far behind, but the finish line is nowhere in sight. The euphoria from the beginning of the run has considerably diminished. Runners have spread out over the course, and there are relatively fewer people around you. This is the time when one can start to feel lonely. This is the time when you have to focus and keep yourself mentally alert and occupied."

I jogged along.

About an hour later, I crossed the 32-kilometer mark. From here on, it was uncharted territory. I had never gone that far in any of my training runs. The sun was up in full force. I still had about 10 kilometers to negotiate. I shrugged.

By the time I crossed 35 kilometers, my state was miserable. I was drenched in sweat, and my calves had cramped up. Each step felt heavier, as if someone was progressively adding ankle weights to my feet. I could feel blisters developing underfoot. Every single body part, even my earlobes, seemed to be aching (yes, that's possible!). I was even learning about a few parts that I never thought existed. But now I knew they did, as they suddenly started filing complaints. I had never ever experienced that kind of physical discomfort.

And then, like clockwork, the inner dialogue started.

me: *"Why the hell are you doing this to yourself? You should stop now. It's okay."*

No response.

me: *"It was never a good idea to transition from a half marathon to a full marathon so quickly. Didn't I tell you that?"*

No response.

me: *"It's okay. On some days, you win, and on others, you learn."*

ME: *"I am in no mood to learn today. So, please shut up."*

I kept chugging along and reached 40 kilometers a short while later. I had come too far to quit now, but I was struggling to find the ammunition to go any further.

I saw a supporter holding the placard that read, "Just two more to go."

The word "just" brought a smile to my face. Given the state I was in, I felt "gigantic" would have been more appropriate.

I remembered the famous quote from Martin Luther King Jr:

"If you can't fly, then run. If you can't run, then walk. If you can't walk, then crawl. But no matter what, keep moving forward."

If there ever was a moment when I needed to derive inspiration from that quote, it was right then. Flying, running, and walking were out of the question. Crawling was the option that I was not willing to give up on, no matter what.

When you run out of strength, your stubbornness can still carry you forward.

So, crawl I did.

Thud. Thud. Thud. Thud ...

I kept putting one foot ahead of the other.

After what felt like an eternity, I saw the finish line in front of me. It was just 100 meters away. "Marathoner Sundeep" was waiting. A tear trickled down my face, and I didn't try to hold it back. No one would have seen it anyway as it was camouflaged in sweat.

And then, in a burst of raw instinct, I sprinted.

I crossed the finish line like a man possessed. A blur of fatigue, emotion, and disbelief.

The journey, or should I say misery, had lasted 4 hours, 14 minutes, and 27 seconds.

There was pain. There was exhaustion. There were blisters. There were tears. But there was more: I was now, officially, a marathoner.

Running the first full marathon in many ways is a discovery process: a process of discovering your true self!

Key Messages

i. **Sometimes, you have to leap before you're ready.**
Not every decision needs a spreadsheet. Some just need a jolt of instinct. In my case, I didn't overthink while signing up for my first full marathon. I just did it—somewhat impulsively, irrationally, and maybe even irresponsibly. But here's the thing: If I had waited to feel "ready," I might never have done it. Some of life's biggest moves aren't made after careful deliberation. They're made in raw moments of instinct, when something inside you says, "Go". And that voice is often wiser than you think.

ii. **The toughest battles are rarely visible.**
During the race, muscles cramp, lungs burn, and the body endures all kinds of discomfort. Yet, the deepest fatigue is often silent. It's that battle inside the head. It doesn't show up on the track, but it whispers every time you face uncertainty, deal with failure, or try to build something new. I've realized that resilience isn't about silencing that voice. It's about not believing it and taking that all-important next step.

iii. **Growth often begins where comfort ends.**
That first race broke me open. Physically, yes, but more so emotionally. I had tasted something difficult, and weirdly, I wanted more. It was the first time I realized that discomfort can be a doorway—that exhaustion, uncertainty, and pain are not signs to stop, but invitations to grow. I haven't looked at struggle the same way since.

4

GOLD STANDARDS DON'T COME EASY

The goal that changed it all

THE renowned Japanese concept of Ikigai offers a framework for finding one's purpose, a reason to get out of bed every morning. It asks you to reflect on four things:

(i) What do you enjoy?
(ii) What are you good at?
(iii) What does the world need?
(iv) What can reward you?

The first time I came across this idea, I was skeptical. It sounded a little too idealistic. One magical pursuit that checks all of those boxes? It felt like a philosophical TED talk waiting to be debunked.

But the year gone by had begun to shift something in me.

I had accidentally wandered into the world of running, and it gave me more than just a workout. It gave me a rhythm, a release, a reason. I couldn't say I had found my Ikigai. But for the first time, the pursuit had begun. I had a firm answer to the first question.

Purpose gradually unfolds. It doesn't announce itself. Often, it starts with a feeling, not a plan.

I enjoyed running.

Plus, it was motivation enough for me to get out of bed early every morning, literally.

Unlike many of my runner friends, I have always been a solo runner. I'd much rather be out at 4:00 a.m., jogging through the still, sleepy roads of Gurugram than coordinate logistics to join a running group. But that didn't mean I didn't enjoy the attention.

Running was giving me a new identity too.

Yes, I was a consulting professional.

Yes, I was a blogger.

But increasingly, people around my society had started recognizing me as *"The tall Sardar who runs."*

When I trained in the evening, little kids would wave at me, cheerfully shouting, *"Running Uncle!"*

I didn't mind it. In fact, I loved it.

That small ripple of recognition, of being known for something outside the usual job-title box, was strangely energizing. I felt seen. And that made me want to raise the bar.

Only, I wasn't sure what "raising the bar" meant in the world of amateur running. So, I turned to the one person who might have a clue: Anubhav at the gym.

"Here comes the marathoner," he said, grinning as I walked in.

"I want to ask you something," I said.

"Of course. Shoot."

"What is the gold standard in recreational running?" I asked.

"What do you mean?"

"I mean, once you've done a marathon, what do people aspire for next?"

Anubhav smiled, that knowing kind of smile you see on a teacher's face just before they drop a quiet truth.

I continued to stare at him in anticipation.

"Accomplished runners often aim for the Boston Marathon."

"The Boston Marathon! What's the big deal?"

"It is the oldest marathon event in the world. And unlike most other events, you can't just sign up. You have to qualify. It's often referred to as the Mecca of amateur running."

"Interesting. How do you qualify?"

"You have to run a qualifying race and complete a full marathon within a certain time limit based on your age group."

"Will my current timing of 4 hours and 14 minutes get me in?"

Not intending to dampen my spirit, Anubhav evaluated his words carefully before responding.

"Yes. If you hold that pace till you are over 70 years old."

"Wait, what?" I asked, confused.

"The Boston Marathon recognizes that running is an age-sensitive sport, so it adjusts qualifying standards for age. Your current timing aligns with the qualifying standard for men in the 70–75 years category."

"Okay, so what's the target for my current age bracket?"

"About an hour faster than your current time. 3 hours and 10 minutes."

"WHAT? That's ... that's insane."

"No one said gold standards come easy."

I stood quietly for a few seconds, letting that sink in.

That was the genesis of a new desire, one that was going to stay with me for a very long time. I was not sure if I could ever qualify for the Boston Marathon, but I was excited about the prospect of chasing the gold standard in the world of amateur running.

The goal had changed.

And that changed everything.

"One day I will get there, Sir," I whispered, almost to myself.

And I walked out, chasing something new.

Real joy often lies in chasing what feels just beyond your reach.

Key Messages

i. Small joys often lead to big purposes.

Running didn't begin as a grand purpose for me. It was just something I looked forward to, a quiet rhythm that made me feel alive. That was enough. I've come to believe that having something you genuinely enjoy isn't a luxury—it's an essential. It could be anything—writing, baking, walking, dancing, thinking, analyzing—anything that makes your heart feel lighter. Find it. Hold on to it. Do a little of it every day. That small joy often leads to something bigger.

ii. Recognition isn't vanity; it's fuel.

When kids called me "Running Uncle," it made me smile. It reminded me of who I was becoming day by day. We often dismiss recognition as ego-stroking. But sometimes, being seen differently is what helps you see yourself differently. And that can be a powerful push to raise your own standards.

iii. Gold standards shift the game.

The moment I heard about the Boston Marathon, something clicked. It wasn't just a race; it was a symbol of excellence, a benchmark that demanded more. I didn't know if I'd ever qualify, but the idea of chasing that goal gave my journey new energy. Sometimes, the real value of a goal isn't in achieving it, but in what it awakens within you.

THE MORE I RUN, THE MORE I LEARN

(2015–2017)

"Life will give you whatever experience is most helpful for the evolution of your consciousness. How do you know this is the experience you need? Because this is the experience you are having at this moment."

—Eckhart Tolle

5

YOU CAN'T POUR INTO A "FULL" CUP

When your thoughts outpace you

I'VE always loved spring—the blooming flowers and chirping birds, that fresh, earthy scent, and the explosion of color. Everything about the season feels like God's personal way of reminding us to smile. It's a season that doesn't try to impress; it just quietly shows up and spreads joy.

After completing the SCMM in January 2015, I found myself eagerly looking forward to the onset of spring, both seasonally and symbolically. I was entering what I can now call the most beautiful phase of my running journey.

The hard part was over. I had become a marathoner—slow, yes, but a marathoner nonetheless. Age was on my side. The road ahead felt long, open, and entirely mine to explore.

I wanted to experience everything that running had to offer: hill runs, trail runs, treadmill runs, fun runs, ultra runs, charity runs, commercial runs, and festive runs; I didn't want to miss a single flavor on the menu. And yes, the dream of qualifying for Boston was quietly parked at the back of my mind. That goal still felt distant, but it was enough to keep the fire going.

I was falling in love—with the road, the rhythm, and the version of myself that showed up to run.

Everyone even remotely close to me knew it.

However, there was something more, something deeper I hadn't spoken about much. At a personal level, I had begun to enjoy something I hadn't expected: my thoughts.

The more I ran, the more aware I became of the inner dialogue I never acknowledged earlier. Thoughts I didn't know I had. Truths I hadn't fully faced. Desires I hadn't dared to voice. Running had become this strange, safe space where every thought—no matter how absurd, inconvenient, random, or *unacceptable*—was welcome.

> *Understanding yourself begins with the simple act of acknowledging your thoughts.*

Running felt like entering a zone where I didn't have to judge myself. I could just *be*. No filters. No masks. Just me.

The good thoughts, the bad ones, the irrelevant ones, the socially awkward ones, the wildly inappropriate ones—all were treated with the same gentle poise by my moving feet.

Sometimes, I'd find myself smiling mid-run, laughing at the absurdity of a thought I'd never admit to in public. There was something beautifully liberating about it. I wasn't trying to find answers, but running kept nudging me toward them anyway.

Over the next year, I became a regular at just about every running event in Delhi: the Delhi Heritage Half Marathon, the Potpourri Run, the Super Sikh Race, Puma Urban Stampede,

Dwarka Half Marathon, and many more. Each event had its own vibe, community, and quirks. Some had traditional music. Some had DJs. Some handed out bananas at the 10-kilometer mark. Some awarded medals shaped like lions or monuments or musical notes.

Yet, underneath all the differences, there was one thread that connected them: the element of joy. Pure, unfiltered joy. Of movement. Of community. Of showing up.

I had no idea where the path was taking me. But I was happy just being on my way.

July 2015

It had been over a year since I started running. My expectations of myself started to evolve. I was no longer content with just finishing the run and flashing my participation medal. With every run, I wanted to run faster. I was beginning to get obsessed with my run timings. Every event was now an opportunity to achieve a new personal best (often referred to as PB in running parlance).

I had also started to become judgmental about other runners around me.

Faster runners were greater runners ...

Slower runners were lesser runners ...

Runners too active on social media did not qualify as runners ...

... and so on.

I don't know when and how these thoughts creeped in. Maybe they were always there, buried, waiting for the right stage to emerge. Perhaps it was the Boston dream whispering in my ear, raising the stakes. Or maybe running was just holding up a mirror, and I was finally seeing myself without the filters.

I had also developed a simple mechanism to deal with thoughts that running introduced me to. I would acknowledge them and move on. I did not have to discuss them with anyone except Japneet. She was my ever-patient sounding board. I'd talk to her for hours about the random, often ridiculous, thoughts that bubbled up during my runs. She'd listen politely and nod, sometimes amused, at other times surprised, always loving me the same way—without judgment. Her quiet acceptance was my safety net.

But back to running.

In the hope of achieving a new PB, I considered signing up for the Day Breaker Half Marathon. The race was scheduled for late July, right in the thick of the monsoon.

And I hated running in the rain.

My simple rule was to abort the run as soon as it started raining, even if it was just a gentle drizzle. I never understood runners who claimed to enjoy running in the rain. In my head, they were just being dramatic. I had strong views about them—just as I did about everything else around me. I considered them foolhardy.

So, I was hesitant to register. What if the rain slowed me down? What if I couldn't beat my last PB? In the newly constructed world inside my head, a slower run meant being a lesser runner. I wasn't sure if I wanted to risk that.

I reluctantly signed up for the marathon anyway.

Arrogance on the run

Days rolled by until the event was just a week away. In the last few days, I would get up and check the weather forecast every morning. I needed ideal conditions: dry roads, cool air, low humidity—anything but rain. I wanted to get a new PB after all. Unfortunately, the forecast did not look great. High humidity and possible rain showers were predicted for race day.

Sunday morning: Race day

Anubhav and I reached the venue around 5:00 a.m. I occupied a quiet corner near the start line and started with my usual warm-up drills. A few minutes before the race flag-off, I walked over to him for one last dose of wisdom.

"Anubhav, I really want to register a new PB today. You know I've trained hard for it. What do you think?"

He leaned in and whispered, "Today is not the day for PB. It's very humid. Don't push too hard. Focus on completing the run safe and strong."

"Roger that, Captain!" I said with a grin. I didn't mean it. Not one bit.

The race started.

Barely 2 kilometers in, it began to rain. My first instinct was to stop, just as I always did. But this time was different. It was a proper running event. I thought about it for a moment.

"I am not stopping today," I whispered. I decided to be foolhardy.

Despite all my aversion, I continued running in the rain.

And something unexpected happened.

The rain, which I had always disliked, felt strangely liberating. The cool droplets, the breeze against my face, the splash of puddles, the scent of wet earth—it was like being a child again. I was soaked, but I was smiling. And just like that, I had a new perspective.

Once the rain stopped, I shifted my focus back to my mission of securing a new PB.

By the halfway mark, everything seemed to be clicking. The pace seemed fine, my body felt good, and a quick calculation confirmed I was on track.

"Who cares about heat and humidity when there is a PB at stake!" I thought, feeling good about my ability to push through difficult conditions. My thought was underpinned by a bit of

pride and a lot of arrogance. Sure, I was feeling strong in the way I was running, which is where the pride came from. But there was a problem. I was feeling a tad too strong—almost invincible—transcending external conditions. Despite all the regard I had for my friend Anubhav, in that moment, I was condescendingly thinking about the suggestion he had offered me prior to the run.

"Today is not the day for PB," I replayed his words in my mind and then went on to build an imaginary response: *"Today may not be a day for PB for the masses, but that doesn't include me, Sir. Things work a bit differently when you train as hard as I do."*

Around the same time, as if it were God's way of preventing me from jumping to a hasty conclusion, things started to change.

The sweating intensified. My legs got heavier. Breathing became labored. The sense of flow evaporated.

And then, the overtaking started.

First one runner passed me. Then another. Then another. And then, I stopped bothering.

By kilometer 16, I was a mess.

Every step was a wet, sloshing drag. My shoes felt like they'd absorbed the Arabian Sea. As a final desperate attempt to revive the run, I took off my T-shirt. I thought that with the amount of sweat it had soaked, just taking it off and squeezing out the sweat would probably make me carry a kilogram lesser. But that was not going to help. I had already screwed the race with the way I ran in the first half, completely condoning Anubhav's advice.

The more I know, the more I realize how much I don't know.

Eventually, I crossed the finish line. Quietly. Without fanfare.

I glanced back to check if I was the last one. I couldn't see anyone behind me. Maybe they'd all already crossed. Maybe I just didn't care anymore.

I grudgingly accepted the verdict for the day.

I found a quiet spot near the finish line and sat down, letting the discomfort settle. And in that silence, a memory resurfaced—a story from my schooldays.

A disciple once approached his master in search of wisdom. However, every time the master tried to explain something, the disciple interrupted, eager to share his own ideas. The master, noticing this, began to pour tea into the disciple's cup. He kept pouring even as it overflowed. The disciple uncomfortably watched it for a while before finally reacting, "Stop it. Can't you see the cup is full? No more can go in." The master replied, "Exactly! You are like this cup. Come back when you have some empty space in you."

That day, I was the disciple.

My cup had been too full of pride, assumptions, and certainty.

I told my friends that I had been undone by the weather conditions, but deep within, I knew that was not true. I had been undone by my arrogance and unwillingness to learn.

Key Messages

i. Your thoughts are your mirror. Observe them closely.

Running gave me access to a part of myself I had never met before. Strange, inconvenient, even inappropriate thoughts surfaced—not to torment me, but to show me who I was. There's a strange peace in letting your mind speak without judgment. You don't always need to solve or suppress your thoughts. Sometimes, acknowledging them is enough.

ii. **Always keep some space in your cup.**
That old story about the overflowing cup came back to me when I needed it most. I had been full of assumptions, judgments, and ego, with no room left to learn. You can't grow if you're already convinced that you know it all. Whether you're running a race or moving through life, keep a little room in your cup. That space is where wisdom enters.

iii. **Life doesn't care who you *think* you are.**
You can walk into a race with your medals, timings, and Instagram-worthy moments. But the road will meet you as you are, not as who you think you are. On that rainy day, the run stripped away my ego and reminded me that performance does not come from self-image. It comes from preparation, presence, and humility. This holds not just for the race on track, but for the race of life.

iv. **Not all growth is visible.**
For a while, I equated growth with better timings. But the real progress was happening elsewhere: in my mindset, awareness, and humility. Some of the most important transformations in life don't necessarily show up in the usual metrics. They show up in how you respond to discomfort, how you treat others, and how honest you are with yourself when no one is watching.

6

HAPPINESS IS A MATTER OF CHOICE

When enough wasn't enough

February 2016

We humans are hungry creatures.

No matter how much we have, we always crave more: more wealth, more recognition, more fame, more success, more peace, more satisfaction, more of just about everything worth having, and sometimes more of things not worth having too.

For long-distance runners, this craving manifests in two forms: Either we want to run longer or we want to run faster.

And in that pursuit of *more*, we get so consumed by the outcome that we miss the joy that lies quietly along the way.

I wasn't immune to this syndrome.

In fact, I had become a classic case study in what you might call *TOMO: Target-Only Mindset Obsession*. I had started getting a real kick out of chasing faster run times, so much so that I completely forgot how far I had come.

From being a couch potato to running marathons.

From struggling to finish 5K to collecting medals at half marathons.

The pursuit of more can blind us to the beauty of enough.

In two years, I had transformed. That alone should have been reason enough to celebrate. But I wanted more. Much more.

It had been over six months since I ran my personal best: 92 minutes in a half marathon. I had now set my sights on a new milestone: the elusive sub-90-minute finish. Among amateur runners, breaking 90 minutes in a half marathon is considered a respectable achievement, one of those informal badges that elevates your status in your own head, if not in the community at large. I wasn't far, and I was itching to get there.

So, I signed up for a half marathon at the Buddh International Circuit in Noida, the F1 track. A few friends who had run it earlier said it was a good place to clock fast times because it was smooth, flat, and wide.

In the lead-up to race day, I did my research. I made two key changes to my running plan.

First, I decided to run without music. It was a big decision. I loved my running playlists, but some experienced runners had told me that music could mess with your rhythm. They said that it throws off the natural sync between breathing and footwork. Second, I promised myself I wouldn't keep checking my watch. Somewhere along the way, I'd picked up the habit of glancing at my pace every few minutes. It didn't help. It only added pressure.

Happiness is a choice, not a chase

Race day

It was still dark when we started lining up at the start line.

Since I was not carrying music, I could hear the hum of conversation, the shuffle of shoes, and the faint rustle of nervous energy in the air. I made a conscious effort to stay focused.

There was a serious mission ahead of me, that of running a half marathon in under 90 minutes—my sweet little worthless mission, dramatically blown out of proportion to elevate the grandeur of my achievement if and when I eventually got there.

The run started at 6:00 a.m. sharp.

"Come on, Champ. Under 90 minutes today," I whispered and took off.

As the kilometers rolled by, I had a strong urge to stare at my watch. I resisted the temptation. Looking at the watch was not part of the plan. "Plans ought to be adhered to," I kept reminding myself.

I finally succumbed to the temptation after running for almost an hour. I was in for a surprise. I had covered 14 kilometers in just under an hour. A sub-90-minute finish was certainly on the cards. I turned to look at the fellow runners behind me. Again, I was in for a sweet surprise. I was leading the race with a sizeable lead.

"That's the way," I shouted and continued to push through.

Around 30 minutes later, I crossed the finish line. I had bettered my PB by over a minute but had missed the 90-minute ambition by around 40 seconds. I also managed to secure first position in the race, my first ever in a competitive run.

I vividly remembered the last time I had secured first position. It was way back, during my Nursery grade. Yes, in those days, schools used to publish ranks even for Nursery students. My sister had been particularly ecstatic as she joyfully jumped up and down while sharing the news with the family. A smile flashed across my face as I compared the two somewhat similar, yet vastly different, and both equally inconsequential performances. Even as I reflected upon the sweet childhood memory, a part of me continued to sulk over the fact that I had missed the 90-minute timing.

A few moments later, a fellow runner approached me.

"Hey Sundeep, congratulations on winning the race!"

"Thanks!"

"I saw you at one of the turns along the route. You were flying!"

"Thanks, buddy."

He looked at me, confused by my flat tone.

"You don't look happy! I thought you won the race?"

"Yes, I did. But ..."

Brief pause.

"But what?" he asked, bewildered.

"But I wanted to finish in under 90 minutes, and I missed that by 40 seconds."

He burst into laughter, "Come on! You won the damn race! This moment won't come every day."

"If I were you, I would really enjoy this moment," he patted my back and jogged away. I stood there, watching him disappear into the crowd of glowing, happy runners.

> *You're only here for a short visit. Don't hurry. Don't worry. And be sure to smell the flowers along the way.*

It may have been a short conversation with a complete stranger. But his words hit me harder than my finish time. They got me thinking.

We're so quick to discount the things we once dreamed of. We obsess over the next milestone, forgetting to honor the one we just crossed. We chase seconds and stats and split times, while the joy quietly slips through the cracks.

A few years ago, if someone had told me I'd one day win a race, I would've leaped with joy. But here I was, brooding over a technicality, sulking over seconds and missing the moment.

"What's wrong with you? You really need to get your act right," I found a part of me shouting at myself.

As more runners arrived at the finish line and conversations picked up, I began to smile again. Not because I ran fast. But because someone had slowed me down just enough to notice the moment I was about to miss.

Whenever someone asked me about the run thereafter, my reply was simple.

"I won the race ..." (... and there was no *"but"* after that!)

Feeling grateful after winning the Buddh International Circuit Half Marathon in Noida

Key Messages

i. The goalpost always shifts, but joy doesn't have to.

What starts as a personal dream can quickly turn into a performance trap. That finish line was more than a physical marker. It was a fleeting opportunity to feel joy, pride, and gratitude. And I still found myself disappointed—not because I failed, but because I had stopped allowing joy to exist unless it came with a perfect scorecard. Whether in a race or in life, the present offers a gift. You just have to be there to unwrap it.

ii. We are quick to mourn what's missing and slow to honor what has become real.

I was so fixated on the sub-90-minute goal that I nearly overlooked something far bigger: I had *won* the race. How often in life do we let a minor shortfall overshadow a major breakthrough? Learning to honor what *did* happen, instead of mourning what didn't, is a powerful act of emotional maturity.

iii. Cherish the journey, rather than fretting over the destination.

As they say, *"You're only here for a short visit. Don't hurry. Don't worry. And be sure to smell the flowers along the way."* In the end, when you look back at your life, it will come down to being a sum total of all the memories. Make sure to create good ones along the way.

7

IT'S NOT DONE UNTIL IT'S DONE!

The irresistible allure of a tougher race

Summer, 2016

I HAD already participated in several high-profile running events across India and was beginning to crave something more challenging. That's when the idea of signing up for the Airtel Hyderabad Marathon (AHM) first crossed my mind. The race had a reputation for its tough terrain and brutal weather; I'd even heard a story about an accomplished runner fainting on the route a few years ago. I can't vouch for the accuracy of that tale, but it certainly added to the mystique. The allure of testing myself on a tougher course was hard to resist.

I often wondered why my appetite for new experiences had grown so dramatically. Just a few years earlier, I had been perfectly content with my predictable life: Wake up, do the morning chores, head to work, come back home, spend time with family, maybe catch a movie, sleep—and repeat. It was simple. Too simple. And I was happy with it. But somewhere along the way, something had shifted. I don't know what exactly. Maybe it was a midlife crisis. Maybe it was a subconscious search for answers to life's bigger questions. Or maybe I was just overthinking, as I often did. Either way, I found myself constantly drawn to new challenges.

And right now, that challenge was called the AHM.

For almost all of my youth and childhood, I was the studious type, the one who would happily pick a paper and pen to solve mathematics questions. And I thoroughly enjoyed it. I was not a kid anymore. Running at the AHM didn't qualify as a mathematics problem either. Yet, the urge to go back to paper and pen was palpable. Cracking the AHM was certainly a new challenge, and it was time to go back to the drawing board to identify the winning formula. So, as I always do, one fine evening, I sat with a neat little paper and a pen to jot down all I knew about the event.

From everything I'd read and heard, two things were clear. First, the AHM course didn't start and end at the same point. Unlike most flat-route races, there was a significant net elevation gain. Second, the route was dotted with flyovers and rolling hills. And if that wasn't enough, race-day weather conditions were notoriously difficult. Runners often had to brave rising temperatures and oppressive humidity in the later stages of the run.

We strategy consultants love to compress complex ideas into neat-looking frameworks. It's almost like a mental arsenal that one can use to deal with complex challenges. Most business-world frameworks, including Kotler's famous 4P framework, may have emerged from this obsession. So, all I had to do as a strategy consultant (and of course, as a runner) was to overcome Hyderabad's 3H obstacles: hills, heat, and humidity.

Set your success GPS before you hit "start" because wandering aimlessly is exhausting.

We consultants also love to define what success looks like before commencing a pursuit. It helps put one's efforts and actions into perspective. To me, it is akin to acquiring a compass that constantly points one in the right direction. I wondered what would qualify as a strong performance at the AHM. I didn't want to be delusional. I didn't want to be too conservative either, for there is no joy in a pursuit that doesn't push you hard enough.

I called up an experienced runner friend for his perspective. After we had talked for over an hour, he neatly summarized it for me, "AHM race timings tend to be 10–15 minutes slower than the usual flat-track races. So, if you haven't yet managed to complete a half marathon in 90 minutes, then running the AHM in 100 minutes would be a big deal."

"Running the AHM in under 100 minutes would be a big deal." I continued to think about his final remark through the day. I liked the sound of that. It excited me. It also scared me. A part of me wanted to mentally sign up for it, but the other part, the devil's advocate, was holding me back.

That night, as I turned off the lights, my two eternal inner voices started their usual bickering.

me: *"You always encourage your colleagues at office to set SMART targets. Don't you?"*

ME: *"Yes, I do. So?"*

me: *"So, do I need to remind you what a SMART target is? It is specific, measurable, achievable, relevant, and timebound!"*

ME: *"I know that. What's the point?"*

me: *"The point is that what you're aspiring for is a bit too ambitious. Don't you think you are not yet ready for a sub-100-minute AHM?"*

ME: *"I know it will be a stretch, but there is no joy in doing things that don't push you."*

me: *"There is a fine line between being ambitious and being absurd."*

The debate was going nowhere, so I did what I often do in such moments: I set an early alarm and decided to mute both voices.

The next morning, before I stepped out for the morning run, I signed up for the event. It was scheduled for the end of August, and I had a good four months to train. I was thrilled.

There is something exquisite about laying your eyes on a goal and following a diligent process to get there. While the goal itself is often pursued in a short window on a particular day (on the race day, for instance), its beauty lies in the meaning it lends to the countless moments leading up to that moment. Beating the alarm every single morning, overcoming food cravings in those weak moments, prioritizing stretching over scrolling—the list of the mini-battles you fight is endless. The whole day is filled with countless mini-victories that bring to life the winner in you. I was falling in love with that joyous feeling. Without realizing it, I was subtly learning the art of living a purposeful life. The purpose itself didn't need anyone's endorsement or validation. Whether or not I achieved a sub-100-minute finish at the AHM would not make any difference to anyone, including me. Yet, it was important to me, important enough to be the single-most critical consideration that defined how I would spend all my time leading up to the race day.

A true goal doesn't just wait at the finish line. It walks with you every day, illuminating the path all along.

In the months that followed, I was obsessed with the desire to run the AHM in less than 100 minutes. I trained hard, significantly harder than ever before.

I added uphill runs to prepare for the terrain. I began training during peak heat hours to acclimatize myself to race-day weather. I even introduced weighted-vest runs on weekends to build leg strength. Running with a 10-kilo jacket made me feel like a commando on a covert mission.

I was happy with the way I was preparing, but a nagging thought always bothered me. I was conscious that all my training was concentrated across a few hours of workout time during the week.

"Can I do something when I am not explicitly training?" I kept thinking all the time.

I eventually had an idea that became an integral part of the way I trained for the AHM. I started wearing light ankle weights to the office every day. Wearing those weights (beneath the socks) meant that with every step I took, my legs were becoming a tad stronger. I would merrily skip the lift and walk up 10 floors to reach my office or walk around the bay once inside the office, with the conviction that every step was getting me closer to my target of a sub-100-minute finish at the AHM. Training wasn't a part of my day anymore. It was my day.

The event was just a day away now. Having trained hard (and a bit unconventionally), I was reasonably confident of breaching the 100-minute timing at the AHM.

Close enough isn't really close enough

As I boarded the flight to Hyderabad, I found my mind wandering. *"Maybe I should have done some more hill runs or more strength training for my legs. I'm narrowly going to miss it,"* I thought. I closed my eyes and made a conscious effort to control the thought-storm brewing within me.

I went to bed early that night. I kept tossing for a long time before eventually falling asleep. Things have a way of showing up in your dream feed when you keep thinking about them all the time. If there was one thing that had really consumed me during those days, it was the AHM. No wonder it featured in my dream that night. I saw that somehow my shoelace had become unmanageably long—about a meter long—and I couldn't tie it even after the race had started. It was one of those nasty nightmares that felt terribly real. I got up with a shudder and picked the shoe lying next to my bed. It was exactly the way it was supposed to be, all set to be taken around the beautiful roads of Hyderabad in a few hours. I was relieved.

I tried to sleep again, but that was not going to be easy. There was too much restless energy that I was struggling to control. After trying for some time, I gave up and decided to get straight to the venue. That was the easiest way to settle the butterflies in my stomach.

I reached the venue a good two hours before the start time. There was hardly anyone at the ground. I had all the time in the world to warm up and get ready for the run.

The route promised to be an interesting one too. For a first-time visitor to Hyderabad, the racecourse doubled up as a scenic city tour, encompassing Hussain Sagar Lake, Banjara Hills, and Jubilee Hills. It was the hop-on-hop-off tour I never signed up for, except I was hopping on my own feet.

Once the race began, I found myself humming an old rhyme from school: *"Fire on the mountain, run, run, run..."* Every time a hill appeared, it felt like a secret dare. And each time, I pushed forward with purpose. I joyfully marched along, managing to hold a good pace.

It had been over an hour and a half since the race started. I was approaching the end of the race. I was about a kilometer away from the famous Gachibowli Stadium, where around 10,000 runners were headed to cross the finish line on that bright and sunny Sunday morning. I nervously looked at my watch. I still had about five minutes to go to finish the run in under 100 minutes.

"That should be enough to knock off this last kilometer," I thought.

My chest swelled with pride. In a moment of premature self-glorification, I dropped the guard.

"The AHM in less than 100 minutes: done and dusted!" I whispered punching the air with joy. That final kilometer became a victory lap in my mind. I slowed down, savoring the moment, basking in my own imagined glory. The runners around me may have noticed the act, wondering what the fuss was all about. But I couldn't care less. I had worked hard to secure a sub-100-minute finish at the AHM, and I was within striking range of achieving that. I was ecstatic already.

What I had momentarily forgotten was that the half-marathon distance is about 100 meters more than 21 kilometers (it is 21.1 kilometers), and those final few meters take some time too. The sub-100-minute finish was gradually slipping away without my realizing it.

Just moments before I crossed the finish line, I saw the watch crossing the 100-minute mark.

I'd missed it. By 10 seconds.

The air punch, the daydreaming, the untimely self-glorification: They had cost me the one thing I had worked so hard for. I wanted to kick myself, but I didn't have the energy. I trudged off the track, bitter and breathless. After doing everything right over the four months leading up to that moment, I'd messed it up in the last few minutes.

Almost there still isn't there. Ask anyone who's narrowly missed a goal.

Later, as I sat quietly in a corner of the stadium, I thought about the infamous Herschelle Gibbs drop in the cricket World Cup in 1999. During that match, Australia and South Africa were fighting for a berth in the World Cup finals. Australia was chasing a target of 214 runs. At a critical juncture in the match, the Australian batsman Steve Waugh hit a ball that went straight to the South African fielder, Herschelle Gibbs. It was a gigantic moment in the match. Gibbs caught the ball, but in an attempt to celebrate too soon, he juggled the ball and dropped it. He had probably dropped the World Cup. Steve Waugh went on to score an unbeaten 120 to guide his team to win the World Cup. Over 26 years later, South Africa is still searching for its maiden World Cup victory.

My missed milestone wasn't a World Cup final, but in that moment, I understood exactly how Gibbs must have felt.

"It's not done until it's done" was the final thought that crossed my mind before I left Gachibowli Stadium.

Moments before crossing the finish line at
Airtel Hyderabad Half Marathon

Key Messages

i. **Purpose gives shape to every step.**
There's something transformational about chasing a personal goal that nobody else may fully understand. The pursuit itself becomes a quiet revolution—not because the world is watching, but because you are. Whether it is running a race or showing up in life, it is the process—the early alarms, skipped lifts, and micro-decisions—that slowly sculpts you into someone you weren't before.

ii. **Almost is not the same as done.**
Finishing strong requires a discipline of its own. There's always a temptation to start celebrating when you are almost there. But being almost there is not the same as being there. Life, like running, doesn't reward intentions; it rewards follow-through. Even a few seconds of distraction can undo several months of diligence.

iii. **You win on some days; you learn on others.**
Missing the mark, especially after doing everything right, teaches you in a way success never can. But it also reveals your character—your ability to reflect, recalibrate, and rise again. I didn't lose because I wasn't capable; I lost because I let my focus waver. And in that moment, I learned something far more enduring: the hunger to do it right next time.

8

THINK YOU CAN OR YOU CAN'T? EITHER WAY YOU'RE RIGHT

When running became a Lego puzzle

AFTER the AHM run, I found myself sulking for days. I was particularly irked at myself for blowing the race through my stupidity. That familiar hollow feeling returned, the one I had experienced after my first half marathon. Over the past few years, this feeling had become a regular guest after every race. I began to wonder what had changed in me. Why did I feel this relentless need to have another event on the horizon all the time?

Addiction to anything is bad, they say. Was I getting addicted to running? Or maybe, it was something very different. Maybe running was not an addiction, but a manifestation—a manifestation of a deep-rooted personality trait that always required me to have a challenge to face. In school, this need was well served through competitive examinations. In college, my obsession with good grades kept me productively occupied.

After the academic life, though, there was a sudden void that I struggled to make sense of for several years. And then, I accidentally stumbled into the world of running, which had the potential to infinitely serve my need for challenges. The more I thought about it, the more I was convinced that it was a personality trait.

Whatever it was, I needed to break my chain of negative thoughts. I needed something new to chase. I considered commencing serious training to qualify for the Boston Marathon. That had been a long-standing dream anyway. For me, it was the ultimate goal as a recreational runner, almost akin to scaling the mountaintop. I wondered if I was ready for the final summit, though. The honest answer was that I was not ready yet. I still had some way to go; I still had to reach the base camp before entertaining the aspiration of scaling the summit.

So, I began wondering what an appropriate running target equivalent to reaching the base camp might be.

The Boston qualification (BQ) criterion for my age category required me to run a full marathon in under 3 hours and 10 minutes. Given that most runners slow down in the second half of a full marathon, I figured I needed to consistently run half marathons in under 90 minutes to even stand a chance.

Now, 90 minutes for a half marathon is a scary number, especially when you've spent more time close to 100 minutes. I gave it another thought. Training for the BQ felt like a formidable task. I wasn't sure if I could do it. It is said that whether you think you can, or you think you can't, you are right either way. I was sure going to be right either way. But I wanted to be right in the right way.

"A half marathon under 90 minutes—that's my next milestone," I whispered. Just saying it gave me a dopamine hit. The gloom started lifting. I instantly felt my brooding shoulders assuming an upright position.

When you want to get to something, there are two things of paramount importance. First, you need to know the winning formula; second, you need to execute it. I was confident of the second part. I was sure that if I knew what it took to do a sub-90-minute half marathon, I would happily do it, no matter how hard it might be. But I was not sure I knew how to do it in the first place. At that time, none of my running friends had managed that timing, so the "phone a friend" option did not exist. I had to find my own winning formula.

At its core, reaching anywhere requires just two things: knowing the path and walking it.

In the hope of finding some direction, I turned to my trusted ally, Japneet. She knew nothing about running, yet my instinct said that the cue I was looking for would come from her.

She listened patiently as I spoke for over an hour, perhaps 90 percent of which was unnecessary context.

"I don't understand the nuances of running. I don't understand the technical details you are talking about. And sorry, I certainly don't know what it takes to run a half marathon in under 90 minutes," she finally said, standing up to leave. I was disappointed. Just before she left, she added, "It feels like a gigantic task. See if you can break it up into smaller components."

She hadn't said anything extraordinary, yet she had inadvertently left me with a cue, the cue that I was searching for: to break the task down like blocks of Lego and then bring it all together.

Out came pen and paper, my old habits. I started building

my little equation. I made a few scribbles and edits, and a short while later, I had three bullet points on the sheet: (i) Distance per step (stride length), (ii) Steps per minute (cadence), (iii) Number of minutes I could run without stopping.

> *Tackle any life challenge like a Lego set: Figure out the pieces, solve them thoughtfully, put it all together.*

It was a Eureka moment for me. I thought I had my hands on a pot of gold in those three bullet points.

Stride length = flexibility. Cadence = cardio fitness. Running duration = muscular endurance.

With that, I had broken up the seemingly gigantic task into smaller components. I was ready to train all over again. And this time, there was a bit more method to my madness.

Flexibility days meant yoga and awkward poses that turned into Instagram-worthy bloopers. Cardio days were filled with jumping jacks, plyometrics, and enough burpees to question my life choices. Strength days meant weights, squats, and the occasional accidental grunt that made the neighbors worry. In between all of that, I continued to run: long slow runs, interval runs, fartlek runs, and the good old "until the playlist ends" runs.

They ask you to trust the process. I was no running expert, and the process I had laid out for myself had no scientific validation. Yet, I completely trusted my instinct, and that allowed me to trust the process.

Long-distance running is not something that you become better at overnight. It's a journey that entails small, incremental gains aggregated over time to be able to see any perceptible improvements. Yet, every morning, I astutely studied myself naked in the mirror to spot any improvements. To my own surprise, I often noticed these improvements. Hilariously enough, I always seemed to know exactly what action brought about that improvement!

"Today, my abs are a bit more visible. I had green tea yesterday. Maybe I should have it more frequently."

"The hamstrings definitely look stronger than yesterday. Surely, it has to be lunges doing the job!"

"My shoulders look more chiseled. It was a good idea to include sprout salad and quinoa in my diet plan."

I was getting obsessed. I was falling in love with myself, and it was a wonderful feeling. There surely couldn't have been any noticeable difference on a day-to-day basis. I was seeing things I wanted to see. I would often joyfully share my observations with Japneet. As a logical individual, she had the license to dismiss my observations as my whimsical fascination. Instead, bless her, on every occasion, she would just smile and say, "You're working so hard. Of course, it's showing."

Maybe I was becoming stronger and faster, even if just a little, with every passing day. I couldn't tell for sure, but the next big event was not too far. I was going to know soon.

Break It Down to Build It Up

As a strategy consultant, I always swore by the power of breaking big, messy problems into neat, bite-sized pieces. But for years, I believed this sacred skill applied only to the world of business and boardrooms. But somewhere along the way, I realized that it is not just management problems that benefit from being broken down. Any problem worth solving—from academic grades to messy relationships, from financial stress to fitness goals—can benefit from this approach.

The moment you stop treating the problem like one giant monster and start dealing with it piece by piece, it starts to look a lot less terrifying.

The first time I applied this technique to a non-management problem was when I used this technique to improve as a runner.

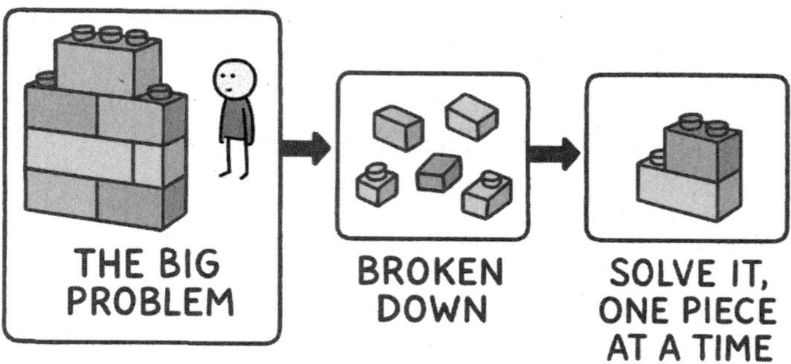

The trick lies in the way we decompose a problem—something that comes with deliberate practice.

Here are a few illustrations:

Illustration 1: I am a **student** trying to improve my grades in school exams. Potential components to consider: • Lack of understanding (didn't grasp concepts) • Insufficient preparation (not enough study or practice) • Inefficient exam strategy (time management, question selection) • Execution errors (careless mistakes) • External factors (health, stress, distractions)	**Illustration 2:** I am a **young professional** trying to figure why my promotion is getting delayed. Potential components to consider: • Skill gaps (technical skills, people skills, etc.) • Inconsistent performance (quality concerns, escalations) • Lack of visibility (senior managers don't know about my impact) • Perception issues (branding, communication gaps)	**Illustration 3:** I am an **adult** navigating a stressful relationship. Potential components to consider: • Communication gaps (misunderstandings, lack of open dialogue) • Misaligned expectations (roles, responsibilities) • Trust issues (past incidents, insecurity) • Lifestyle differences (priorities, goals) • External pressures (work stress, family dynamics)

The day I arrived at the *base camp*

November 2016, Airtel Delhi Half Marathon

As I stood at the start line of the ADHM 2016, memories of my debut half marathon at the same venue two years ago flooded back. I felt a mix of pride and lingering anxiety.

On the one hand, that was a special moment: I was officially christened a long-distance runner at the event. On the other hand, I couldn't stop thinking about my misery toward the end of the run. It was a skeleton dance that would embarrass anyone who claims to be a long-distance runner. I shrugged.

"Regardless of how much time I take to finish the run, I am not going to do a skeleton dance today. I will finish strong," I vowed to myself.

I nervously scanned the sea of runners around me. It was the same vibrancy and energy I had witnessed for the first time in my life two years ago. There was loud music, Zumba, warm-up sessions, runners dressed in fancy colors, and much more. Yes, it was exactly the same. Nothing had changed. It was all familiar to me by now. I had seen enough and more events in the past two years. Yet, I was looking at this event very differently this time. Or maybe, I was not looking at it all, for I was too occupied with my thoughts.

"First kilometer no faster than 4 minutes 45 seconds."

"Ten kilometers within 45 minutes, but not faster than 42 minutes."

"First hydration at the 10-kilometer mark."

"Matches are won or lost in the second half. There's no point getting off to a flying start if that leads to a skeleton dance at the end."

"1-2 breathing pattern today. 1 in, 2 out; 1 in, 2 out ..."

"... and no skeleton dance today, no matter what."

The adrenaline rush was getting the better of me. I had no mind space to observe the vibrancy and celebrations around me. I was on a mission, an inconsequential self-imposed mission to run a sub-90-minute half marathon. It had no relevance to anyone, yet I was treating it like a matter of life and death.

Somewhere along the way, the joy of running had made way for timings, targets, and PBs. It was not that I had any problems with that; I was enjoying it as much as before, but in a very different way. As an ardent student, I couldn't help noticing the shift in perspective and the rapidity with which it had happened. I wondered whether the shift reflected the usual human modus operandi. We often start taking what we have for granted, allowing our mind to crave for what we don't have. It's all in the mind. It's all about how we look at things.

Before I could think any further, the mad rush started. The race was underway.

The first two kilometers are always the trickiest. Yes, matches are won and lost in the second half, but as I started the run, I wondered whether that was entirely true of long-distance running. From experience, I knew that it was possible to lose a long-distance race in the first 15 minutes. Remember my first run? All you need to do is run a little faster than the desired pace, something that happens all the time to novice runners. Such is the frenzy and excitement all around that it is almost impossible to gauge the right pace. It's as if the energy around you creates a mysterious wave that engulfs you, propelling you forward apparently effortlessly. But it turns out to be a mirage a few kilometers later, when you realize that you were burning precious energy reserves all this while, accumulating fatigue that comes back with a vengeance and hits you hard once the frenzy settles down.

Life, like a race, rewards those who pace wisely. Sometimes, holding back early is important to finish strong.

Yes, it's not easy. And I can say that from experience, having screwed God alone knows how many races with the same mistake. Every time, I would come back and promise myself not to press the throttle in the first few kilometers only to do exactly that in my next race, and then the race after that, and then in the race after that too! It's something I never really got right. Even now, over 10 years later, I occasionally struggle with the same mistake.

But ADHM 2016 turned out to be an exception.

I did not get carried away in the first few kilometers. It was probably the horror of the skeleton dance from two years back that stopped me. Once bitten, twice shy perhaps. All I wanted to do was maintain a steady pace, one that I could hold through the run. And I knew it wouldn't happen by chance. I had to do something unusual to get it right. So, something unusual I did.

I whistled my favorite song through the first few kilometers. The rule was to run at a pace that would allow me to sustain whistling. I followed the tactic for the first three kilometers. Every time I felt that the whistling was becoming laborious, I slowed down.

Kilometer after kilometer, I held steady. Controlled. Focused. No theatrics. No unnecessary surges.

I finished the run in 1 hour, 29 minutes, and 39 seconds.

I had finally run a sub-90-minute half marathon.

And for the record, there was no skeleton dance at the end. Just a beaming smile, a quiet fist pump, and the proud knowledge that I had just reached the base camp on the journey to Boston.

Overwriting the unpleasant "skeleton-dance" memory (at the same venue) from two years ago

Key Messages

i. **Sometimes, asking the right question is more powerful than the right answer.**

Not all solutions come from experts. Sometimes, a simple perspective from someone outside the problem can spark a breakthrough. When you're too deep in the details, a fresh pair of eyes can help you see what you've been missing. Japneet wasn't a runner, but her quiet presence and thoughtful nudge helped me unlock what I couldn't see myself. She reminded me that support doesn't always mean offering answers. Sometimes, all it means is helping you ask the right question.

ii. **Break it down to build it up.**

Whatever the challenge—career, relationships, health—what overwhelms us is often not the task itself, but how we look at it. I learned that the best way to deal with something that feels insurmountable is to break it down. When I deconstructed my sub-90-minute goal into stride, cadence, and endurance, it suddenly felt doable. Big dreams become real when you convert them into small, trainable habits.

iii. **Belief is often the first step toward change.**

Progress often begins in the mind, long before it becomes visible in the world. Whether it's a new role at work, healing from heartbreak, or chasing a personal goal, belief is the seed. I saw change in the mirror before it truly existed, but that belief fueled consistency, which over time turned into habit.

9

YOUR DESIRES SET THE UNIVERSE IN MOTION

Tryst with God

IT had been three years since I started running. As I looked back, a lot seemed to have changed, and all for the good. I had undergone a quiet revolution, physically, mentally, and in spirit. The couch potato who got breathless after climbing a flight of stairs was now running sub-90-minute half marathons with surprising consistency. My weight had rolled back to what it was during college, something even my old jeans had stopped believing was possible. Local running events had become a familiar playground. Podium finishes were becoming routine. I was thoroughly enjoying the applause and recognition. That's not what I had started running for, but I did not mind it either.

God had been kind enough to shower this unexpected gift, the gift of running, that could make me happy anytime, anywhere. All I needed to do was put on my sneakers, punch in my ear-plugs, and go.

Yeah, you can be the greatest, you can be the best
You can be the King Kong banging on your chest
You can beat the world, you can win the war
You can talk to God, go banging on his door…

(*Hall of Fame* by The Script)

The beat would go on in a cyclic loop, as I would merrily run long miles listening to the beautiful song. I just couldn't seem to get enough of it.

It was late 2016 when I heard about a new running event in Delhi: The New Delhi Marathon (NDM). What made it special was that none other than Sachin Tendulkar would flag off the event. As a die-hard Sachin fan, I had to be there. I signed up without a second thought. If running had brought me this far, maybe it could also take me closer to one of my childhood dreams: seeing Sachin in person.

February 26, 2017

As I walked into the stadium that morning, my eyes scanned every face. Sachin wasn't there yet. But my mind had already wandered off. I was reliving iconic Sachin moments: the Sharjah storm, the World Cup centuries, the double ton, the desert sixes. As I bent down to tie my shoelaces one last time before the run, I heard a sudden eruption of cheers. The stadium trembled. I didn't need to look up. I knew.

Sachin had arrived.

What I saw next was intense, emotional, nostalgic, and beyond words.

With a large flag in his hand, Sachin stood just a few meters away from me. The fact that I made it to the first few rows from the start line helped me get a good view. The first thing that struck me about Sachin was the radiant glow on his face—a glow that one cannot be born with, that certainly cannot be acquired through the use of cosmetic creams, a glow that one attains through single-minded focus and going through the grind day after day, month after month, for almost 25 years! I felt an intense rush of flashbacks to my younger days. The sight of Sachin had probably nudged the memory blocks, which were now trying to regain equilibrium.

I remembered two very personal Sachin moments. The first was during my college hostel days, when a senior made the mistake of slandering Sachin just after his dismissal in a crucial match. I didn't say a word—I just slapped my senior. One tight, unfiltered, straight-down-the-line slap. That did the job. Respect restored.

The second was on the day of my engagement. Everything was great—a grand banquet hall, top-notch food, an amazing DJ, the company of friends and family—and it all looked impeccable. The only glitch was that the timing of the event coincided with the India versus Australia Final match in the Commonwealth Bank Series. Japneet and I, dressed in our finery, slipped out of our own party to huddle around a TV in a *kirana* store. Sachin scored an unbeaten century and made the auspicious day a bit more special for both of us.

I kept staring blankly at Sachin. Mesmerized.

The run started.

Sachin cheerfully waved at the passing cavalcade. I continued to stand still though, blankly staring at Sachin, even as other runners commenced their run. Sachin and I shared eye contact for the briefest second. He smiled, gave me a thumbs-up, and gestured, *go on*. That was it. That brief moment jostled me out of my reflective state. I was ready to rock 'n' roll.

I started running, not just in the race, but through memories I thought I'd packed away. Each kilometer was a tribute: 1992

Perth, 1998 Sharjah, 2003 Centurion, 2011 Wankhede. The miles flew. The nostalgia soared. The race ended. I crossed the finish line still thinking of other Sachin innings I hadn't yet had time to relive. One tiny half marathon was clearly not going to be enough.

> *The journey gives you more than you seek if you're willing to stay the course.*

In a strange way, running had brought me another unexpected gift, one that I genuinely valued. I wondered whether I got to see Sachin because I started running, or whether I started running because I was destined to meet the great man one day.

When the Boston dream moved from someday to soon

August 2017

Running was giving me so much joy, but I wanted more, much more; it was just that I did not know what "more" meant anymore. I often pondered this question over long-distance runs: "*What do I really want out of my running?*" I never seemed to get a definite answer. Maybe I didn't want anything out of it. All I wanted was it.

There was, however, one goal that still sparkled like an untouched summit: Boston. The coveted BQ. I certainly wanted that.

That evening, after I finished the run, I sat in a quiet spot beneath a banyan tree. I thought about what I needed to do to achieve a BQ. Just then, my phone rang. It was Anubhav.

"Hey, Anubhav! Good to see your call. All good?" I asked, sounding somewhat surprised.

"All good, Sundeep. I called to check in. Where have you been? I haven't seen you in a long time."

"I've been traveling a bit, so I've been in and out of town," I replied.

"I hope running is continuing well?"

"Yes, Sir. That's one thing I don't compromise on, regardless of how hectic things are at work," I said.

We chatted briefly and hung up. I wondered why he'd called. There was apparently no purpose behind that call, or maybe there was one that I hadn't understood. It feels good when someone calls without a reason, without anything to ask for, just like that. With the exception of my family, and probably one or two old college friends, I don't think anyone ever calls me just like that. It felt good to have another friend, who *just* calls.

A few days later, I dropped in at Bomiso. After finishing his workout, Anubhav took me aside. We comfortably sat across two adjacent bench presses as we started chatting. Midway through the discussion, he said something that appeared completely out of context, "I think you are ready to chase the gold standard now," he said.

"Gold standard?!"

"Yes, the gold standard we talked about a few years ago."

"You think I won't have to wait till I turn 70?"

We both smiled.

"With the momentum you have built, you are ready to train for BQ now. I called you the other day to say exactly this, but then I thought it might be better to convey it in person."

It often takes another voice to echo what your heart already knows so you can step forward with confidence.

He then waved at his reception staff to join us. In no time, a small group had gathered around me.

Anubhav continued, "This is Sundeep. He's training for Boston. Make sure that you provide him with all the support he needs to train. He walks in anytime, he walks out anytime, no questions. He shouldn't have to wait for any machine. Just take good care of him."

"What is the next event you have signed up for?" Anubhav asked, turning his attention back to me.

"I am running the ADHM in November 2017, but that's a half marathon. And then I am running the NDM in February 2018, which is a full marathon and a qualifying event for Boston."

"That works very well. By October, let's try to improve your half-marathon timing by a few more minutes, and then in February, let's go for BQ."

"Roger that, Coach!" I grinned.

As I walked back home, my attention turned back to the random call I had received from Anubhav a few days back. They say that when you truly desire something, the universe conspires to help you get there. I wondered whether the call from Anubhav that day was a part of that profound conspiracy to help me secure a BQ. I wasn't sure, but a part of me wanted to believe that it was a sign from the higher power to nudge me in the right direction. Whatever it may have been, I was thrilled.

With Anubhav's support, I was ready to take my training to the next level. There were qualified trainers helping me. What is more, this time around, I was not training for a self-defined whimsical target but for the gold standard. That in itself was huge motivation to push hard, and I couldn't have asked for more.

In the months that followed, I trained like never before. Rain or shine, dawn or midnight, I showed up. I ran, I lifted,

I stretched, I rested, and I logged everything like a man on a mission.

Countdown to glory starts

November 19, 2017, ADHM race day

I was back at my old hunting ground for the fourth year in a row. This time, I was laser-focused. No butterflies. No skeleton dance. Just business. It was an interim milestone en route to the all-important BQ attempt I was going to make in February 2018.

Exactly a year ago, I had been anxiously standing at the start line, hoping to achieve the sub-90-minute timing for a half marathon. This time around, however, that timing was not a consideration. I knew I would comfortably finish the race in less than 90 minutes—it was just a question of how much faster.

I switched on the Garmin watch, raring to go. A few seconds later a message flashed on the watch screen with a beep, "GPS is ready."

"So am I," I murmured, nodding my head.

... and off I went.

Having been there for the previous three editions, I knew the route by heart. There were no unexpected variables. It was a simple uncomplicated drill: Lodhi Garden, India Gate, Parliament Street, Jantar Mantar, U-turn, and the same milestones again before returning to the Jawaharlal Nehru Stadium. No heartbreaks, no surprises—a simple, smooth execution of the race-day plan. Perhaps the only surprise that awaited me was at the finish line.

I finished the race in 1 hour, 26 minutes, and 29 seconds.

Having trained hard, I knew I would finish the race faster than the previous editions, but shaving off over three minutes from my previous best was a pleasant surprise.

After the strong performance at the ADHM, I was curious to know how far I was from the BQ timing of 3 hours and 10 minutes for a full marathon. My hypothesis was that for the full marathon, even if I were to run the second half a bit slower, I could still beat the BQ threshold.

"I won't know until I try," I thought, and decided to run a mock full marathon the same month.

Two weeks later, I returned to my favorite route in Gurugram for what I called my "mock BQ." I wanted it to feel as close to race day as possible, minus the crowds, music, madness, and well, Boston. Japneet had kindly agreed to be my hydration crew, stationed at carefully planned intervals with bottles of electrolytes and an encouraging smile.

The run went well, almost too well. I finished in just over 3 hours and 11 minutes. A solid effort, but still a minute adrift from the elusive BQ mark. Oddly, I wasn't disappointed. After all, it was just a training run without the energy of a real race: no runners to chase, no medal to flaunt at the finish line, and definitely no DJ spinning Bollywood remixes at 6 a.m.

I was happy. For the first time, BQ didn't feel like a pipe dream anymore. I wasn't chasing a distant summit, or so I felt. I could see the peak.

"Stick to the plan, don't do anything stupid, and you've got this," I told myself.

Then, just for good measure, I whispered under my breath, half-shy, half-smug, and completely hopeful:

"Boston, here I come."

Key Messages

i. **Never suppress your innocent desires.**
As Paulo Coelho put it, "When you truly desire something, the whole universe conspires to help you get there." The first time I read it, I found it a bit of an exaggerated claim, but the act of running has made me believe that it is probably true at a divine level. Genuine heartfelt desires do have an uncanny knack of getting enabled by the cosmic powers around us.

ii. **Signs often show up disguised as people.**
Anubhav's casual check-in didn't come with a grand reveal. It was just a friend calling, seemingly without an agenda. But that moment shifted something. Sometimes, people enter our lives right when we need a nudge, a mirror, or a reminder of who we're becoming. They may not even realize it, but they become part of our unfolding journey. Be open. Listen between the lines.

iii. **Growth feels different when you're not chasing, just becoming.**
There comes a point when discipline stops feeling like a grind and starts feeling like grace. You're no longer forcing the pace. You're flowing with it. And the goal isn't out there anymore. It's right here, in the quiet joy of showing up. That's when the process becomes the prize.

NOTHING CHERISHABLE COMES EASY

(2017–2022)

"Courage isn't having the strength to go on; it is going on when you don't have the strength."

—Theodore Roosevelt

10

THE ONLY WAY OUT IS THROUGH

If only there was a trophy for willful denial

February 2018

IF you live in North India, November and December are not the best months for outdoor running. This is the season when a perfect storm of stubble burning, post-Diwali fireworks, and winter fog conspire to produce an annual air-pollution apocalypse. The Air Quality Index (AQI) routinely climbs above 400, making even the boldest outdoor enthusiasts rethink their life choices. Schools are shut, masks become part of everyday fashion, and hospitals brace for an uptick in respiratory cases.

Running outside isn't just inadvisable—it's borderline masochistic. Sensible runners either retreat indoors or take a well-earned break. But I had a BQ to chase.

"This is not the time to slow down. This is the time when I should be running long distances," I thought.

At a time when the rest of Delhi was busy air sealing their homes and shopping for air purifiers, I was out on the roads, clocking long distances through the toxic haze. Ten kilometers. Twenty. Thirty. Even forty. Day after day, I soldiered on through thick smog, trusting my superhero logic, *"What could impact me anyway? I am the invincible warrior. No obstacle can be big enough for me,"* I often thought as I ran through those smoggy winter mornings.

Every few days, I'd skim news headlines warning about pollution-induced health risks. "Delhi's toxic air equals smoking 49 cigarettes a day," screamed one article. The AQI had reportedly crossed 900.

"It can't be that bad," I scoffed, brushing it off as media hyperbole. That's what I told myself—an educated man making an impressively uneducated judgment. If there were a trophy for willful denial, I would probably be a top contender. The perils of air pollution were right in front of me, but I chose ostrich-like ignorance. Just because I was refusing to see the risk, I assumed the risk would not impact me, and there was no visible impact anyway.

> *What we choose to ignore has a way of catching up with us.*

By around the end of December, though, the impact had started becoming apparent. I developed a stubborn cough that refused to leave. At first, I thought it was a viral infection. I took an antibiotic course, but the cough persisted. I began resorting to natural remedies—herbal tea, green tea, gargles, steam, hot water, very hot water, black water, mysterious water—I tried it all. But none of it helped. The cough continued to increase, both in intensity and frequency. By around mid-January, I had reached a state where the cough would occasionally lead to a feeling of choking. It was getting from bad to worse. But remember, I was the superhero, the invincible warrior, and no obstacle could be big enough for me. So, I continued to do my training runs with a few tweaks to my routine—I added a mask, paused mid-run for water breaks during coughing episodes, and then resumed running as if nothing had happened.

By early February, my condition had deteriorated enough to rule out any possibility of training runs. But I still refused to realize the gravity of the situation. The whole world was supposed to be conspiring in *my* favor after all, or at least that's what I thought. Days continued to roll by, but there was no improvement in my cough. If anything, it was worsening. The qualifying race was just days away, and inside my head, the usual suspects were back at it.

me: *"Stop fooling yourself now. There is no way you are going to make it this time around. Just accept that and make peace with it."*

ME: *"I am not going to give up so easily. I did a full marathon in 3 hours and 11 minutes, that too in a casual training run. I am sure to clear the BQ."*

me: *"Yes. If things had stayed on track, you were surely going to do it. But BQs are not achieved coughing and huffing. You need to be at the peak of your fitness."*

ME: *"So, what do you want? You want me to let go of the opportunity to do a BQ after coming so close! Is that what you want?"*

me: *"It's not about what I want or don't want. It's about what's viable. The condition you are in, there is no way you are going to make it."*

ME: *"You're the most consistent naysayer I've ever met!"*

Pause.

me: *"Okay, you go out today and try a run. It's been three weeks since you ran anyway, so some practice won't hurt. If you can get through 5 kilometers without coughing, then go ahead with the full marathon on the race day."*

ME: *"For the first time, you have suggested something that doesn't immediately qualify as trash. I'll take that suggestion."*

Later that day, I stepped out for a casual run. All I needed to do was run 5 kilometers without coughing, and it would secure the license from my cynical self to run the all-important race. The run turned out to be a disaster. I had barely run 700 meters when I had a terrible coughing episode, one that rendered me partially breathless for a few moments. I could feel myself blacking out. I held on to a pole adjacent to the running track, desperately trying to find my next breath. I didn't want to collapse on the track. I have no clear memory of what happened for a few moments after that. All I remember is hearing a few muffled voices that I could not make sense of.

I was not sure for how long I had been holding on to that pole.

"Are you okay?" was the first voice I distinctly remember hearing from amongst a group of people who had gathered around me.

"Yes, yes, 100 percent," I lied, the kind of lie you tell when your pride shows up instead of your better judgment.

"Doesn't look like it, buddy."

Without making eye contact with anyone, I dusted off the embarrassment and slowly walked away. I wondered for how long I had been leaning against that pole and what those people had noticed. I cringed.

The debate around whether to run in the NDM had been well and truly settled. For a change, the two polarized versions, "ME" and "me," were completely synchronized. They were both unhappy, "ME" probably a bit more than "me," but they were unified in their decision to not run in the NDM.

The invincible warrior had finally met his match—not in the form of fatigue or distance, but in a smog-soaked North Indian winter.

I had made peace with the decision not to run, but as the race day drew closer, it stayed on my mind. One of the guiding principles I've always tried to live by is simple: *Show up*. No matter how tough the odds, how cold the morning, or how steep the hill—just show up. This principle has served me well through academics, career, and life at large. So, though I had accepted I wouldn't be running, not showing up at all felt like a betrayal of that belief.

Besides, this wasn't just any event. Sachin Tendulkar, my childhood hero, was once again the brand ambassador. Just a year ago, I'd had my first brush with the great man. This time, even if I couldn't run, the idea of seeing him again was exciting.

Two days before the event, a quiet spark of inspiration struck. I decided to print out a personal note: a collage of my favorite Sachin moments, snapshots of a fan's memory across two decades. If I couldn't chase a timing this year, maybe I could chase this one dream instead—giving that tribute to Sachin.

"If running is not an option, then let me go with the next best option," I excitedly thought.

The most memorable run I didn't run

Race day

The full marathon race was scheduled to start at 4:00 a.m. It was a familiar morning, yet very different: There were no warm-ups or pre-run fueling, just a laminated card in my hand and a childlike hope in my heart.

"Years later, you will feel good about showing up today. Had you decided to sleep through this cold morning, you would have repented later," said a silent self-gratifying voice within me. *"What's the big deal about not being able to run today anyway? Some things are beyond your control, and you can't help it. But at least you did what's in your control. You showed up, and that's what makes you a champion."* I am not sure if I was justified in considering myself a champion even without running the race. But it still felt great to listen to that inner voice.

Doing what you can, even when you can't do it all, is a quiet victory.

I nodded in the affirmative to acknowledge the friendly voice within me. I was conscious that runners around me may notice, so I quickly checked the nod and pretended to be sane.

I found a spot near the barricades and leaned against an ad billboard, watching the pre-race frenzy unfold. A few minutes later, the moment I'd been waiting for arrived. Sachin walked up to the dais.

And just like that, I was gone. Not physically—but mentally, emotionally, and nostalgically transported to another world. I could hear Tony Greig's voice reverberating in my head from almost 25 years ago, "That's gone many a mile! Sachin Tendulkar ... What a player, what a wonderful player!"

I didn't blink. I couldn't. The crowd, the chaos, the runners—everything faded. I just stared, intently watching him wave the flag. As the marathon runners began their journey, I stood still, a spectator this time, not a participant. And strangely enough, I didn't mind.

Running, they say, is a great metaphor for life. The wisdom of this simple sentence was beginning to dawn upon me. My running journey had been a tale of uninterrupted successes and triumphs until that point. The law of averages had to catch up at some point, but the timing was a bit disappointing. Had it happened a few weeks later, I might have qualified for the Boston Marathon. I continued to look at Sachin blankly, holding the small laminated card I was carrying for him. The great man had waited for 22 years to realize his dream of winning the World Cup. There couldn't have been a more appropriate inspiration for me in that moment.

A few minutes later, the full-marathon runners left the start line. The half-marathon kick-off was still about two hours away. That was my window of opportunity. I was not sure how best to approach him, though. There were several security guards fencing the dais.

"Run. The race has started," said a security guard.

"I am not well, so I am not running today."

"Then why are you here?"

"To meet him," I said, pointing to Sachin.

"That won't be possible. If you want to run, go now, or leave," he replied sternly, not trying to hide his frustration.

"I need to give this to Sachin."

"What is this?"

"That's none of your business," I replied, my turn this time to show frustration.

"Give it to me. I will give it to Sir."

"No. I need to …"

Just then, like divine intervention, Sachin looked our way. He was too far away to have heard us, but perhaps he sensed the commotion. He smiled and waved us through.

I walked up to him with a mix of excitement and disbelief. I had planned to say so much, but in that moment, everything evaporated. I stood there, blinking, speechless, drowning in intense nostalgia that arises from the convergence of memories from over two decades into a single moment. The prayers, the butterflies in the stomach, the anxiety, excitement, joy, celebrations, and disappointments—there wasn't an emotion that didn't carry an associated Sachin memory for me.

"Why aren't you running?" he asked, smiling.

"I am not well, Sir."

"Then you should have rested. It's quite cold and early to be out in the open if you are not well," he replied.

"I had to come ... I wanted to meet you," I paused. "And give you this."

He looked at the card, curiosity lighting up his face. "What's this?"

"These are my favorite Sachin memories from over two decades of serious fan-following. I wanted to take the opportunity to give them to you."

"This is very kind of you," replied Sachin, carefully taking the card from my hand. Standing there on the dais, he intently started reading the content.

I was conscious of Sachin's commitments at the event, so I intervened, "Sir, it's a long write-up. You can read it at your leisure, maybe on the flight back to Mumbai."

He smiled heartily and replied, "Okay. I will read it properly when I get back to the room. But thank you so much for this warm gesture. Moments like these always feel so special."

"Thank you!" I replied, dumbstruck by Sachin's humility and the simplicity with which he carried himself.

Just when I thought the moment was over, he surprised me again.

"What do you do with these after the event?" he asked, pointing to the running bib I was wearing on my vest.

"I usually write my timing from the run and keep them in a folder, like a souvenir."

"No timing today," he said. "So, let's write something else."

He took the bib, pulled out a pen, and in his neat left-handed scrawl wrote:

"Keep running. Stay fit. —Sachin."

Of all the running events I had been to, this one turned out to be the most memorable for me, without running a single step.

Sometimes, when you show up without any expectation, you walk away with more than you could've imagined. God has his own pacing strategy. You just need to stay in the race.

> *The moments that move us most often come when we stop trying to control the script.*

Mandatory system upgrade

As a corporate professional, I spend a good part of my day on a laptop. Over the years, I've picked up the terrible habit of never properly shutting it down. Closing the flap feels far too convenient. Open to start, close to stop. Why bother with shutdowns and restarts when you can just snooze?

Even when the system pleads for a reboot to install important updates, I choose to ignore it. It always begins politely: "You must restart your computer to complete the installation of updates."

Two options follow: *Restart now* or *Snooze and remind me again*. I always choose the latter, and like a loyal procrastinator, select the longest snooze duration available. This routine goes on for days until the system finally loses its patience.

Then comes the dreaded message: "Your computer is about to restart."

"No, no, no. Not now!" I cry, smacking my forehead.

The system, unmoved, reboots itself like a cold, calculating monk who warned me long enough and has now renounced all worldly negotiations.

But why am I thinking about this?

Because nature works in eerily similar ways.

Just like Windows, nature expects you to listen to its subtle cues: fatigue, tightness, those little aches and sniffles. If you keep hitting the snooze button on those signals, nature eventually stops asking. And when it does act, it doesn't come with countdown timers. It just pulls the plug, without apology or warning.

That's exactly what happened in my running journey.

I had been running relentlessly for nearly four years, with no breaks, no off-seasons, no "maintenance mode." Be it holidays, festivals, work travel, or illness, I found a way to keep logging my miles. I gave my body no real pause for recovery. It was bound to rebel. So, one fine day, nature said, "Enough," and yanked a mysterious lever: the cough that wouldn't quit.

I once read that humans are "meaning-making" machines. We make meaning by telling stories about who we are and what the events of our life signify. I too was introspecting to make sense of not being able to run at the NDM, at a time when I seemed ready to qualify for the Boston Marathon. The good thing is that as the author of your own story, you have the license to interpret its meaning in the way that makes you happy. If my laptop reboot analogy was anything to go by, it meant that once this system rebooted, I'd return with better software. I just didn't know how long the reboot would take.

Sometimes, life forces a "reboot"—it's your chance to come back stronger and wiser.

With the NDM behind me and no race looming immediately, I had the luxury of time. The next BQ race I was targeting was in January 2019, a full year away. It felt like a rare opportunity to slow down, reflect, and most important, recover. I decided to treat it as a much-needed reboot, both mentally and physically.

For a runner used to high mileage, scaling back felt unnatural. My body had reset its baseline to a fairly high normal, so running once a week felt almost like doing nothing at all. Still, I resisted the urge to do more. With my running volume slashed, I redirected that time to other aspects of wellness: strength training, sleep, nutrition, and mindfulness. My Google search history began to include questions like "What are the best mobility drills?" and "Do beetroot shots actually help?"

It's amazing what a shift in perspective can do. Not long ago, I was sulking over the involuntary break. Now, it felt like it was part of a grander, more transformative plan. And I wasn't just tolerating the break—I was starting to enjoy it.

"Game on. I'll come back stronger," I told myself. "And this time, I'll be ready for Boston."

I stayed committed to rebuilding for several months. I got busy getting stronger and hopefully faster. My cough, stubborn as it was, took its own time to leave. It wasn't until October—seven long months later—that I felt fully recovered. I was ready to resume running, and I was thrilled. When I resumed running, I did it with caution. No outdoor marathons through Delhi's toxic air. Most of my runs were now indoors, on the treadmill. Not as scenic, but far safer.

With three months left for the next qualifying race, the countdown had begun.

Wish life had a *Skip ad* button

January 2019, Tata Mumbai Marathon

As I stood at the start line, I felt ready to complete the unfinished business from the previous year—and this time, I was mature enough to make space for uncertainty. I felt happy but could sense a faint current of sadness weaving its way through me, as if the two emotions weren't opposite at all, but inseparable companions, like two sides of the same coin. It was one of those moments where you feel the full stretch of your emotional spectrum collapsing into a single, indescribable breath.

I looked around. There were thousands of runners around me. All of them probably had a story—some were fully aware of it while others were still discovering it, with running as their compass. They were all chasing something: fitness, peace, friendship, clarity, redemption, joy. There were surely a hundred different pursuits playing out across that sea of bibs and sneakers.

"What am I chasing here?" I wondered.

I let the question linger for a moment, letting it echo inside me.

"A lot of things," I smiled. "But none more so than BQ." That helped me bring my focus back. Philosophical interpretations could wait for another day, I reasoned.

A full marathon is a beautiful beast. Sure, it tests your physical endurance, but what has always fascinated me about the sport is how much your mindset shapes the final outcome. For the same level of physical fitness, two people can land miles apart, depending solely on how they show up mentally. There's so much time to spend with yourself in a marathon, and it's not always a party.

If all went well that day, I was hoping to finish in just under 3 hours and 10 minutes. I recalled the mock marathon I'd done the year before. Back then, I'd finished in 3 hours and 11 minutes (3:11) and felt convinced I was ready to crack the BQ code. This time, though, I wasn't so sure. The layoff, the comeback, the rush to rebuild—it was all still fresh. There was an undercurrent of uncertainty that hadn't existed before.

Three hours is a long time to be spending all by yourself. I thought about ways to engage myself mentally during the run. Just before the race started, a strange idea occurred to me. I thought that at every kilometer mark, I would think about what life used to be at that numerical age. It was an interesting idea, something that I had never tried before. For my contemplative mood that day, the idea carried irresistible appeal. I decided to give it a shot.

The run began.

The idea was novel because it forced me to reflect upon my life in a compartmentalized way. While running each kilometer, I purposefully allowed long-forgotten memories from that numerical age to resurface. I could visualize random memories flashing in front of me, some making me smile, others making me frown, still others making me cry. It was like watching my own movie, over a run! I didn't bother checking my emotions either. I simply allowed the mind to react to what it was "watching." I marched along.

At the midway mark (21.1 km), it felt like I had reached the intermission. It was time to take a short break before resuming the rest of the movie. Of course, this intermission was different from grabbing a bag of popcorn. I glanced at my watch to see how the run was progressing. I had reached the half-way point in about 1 hour and 32 minutes (1:32). I was feeling okay; there were no red flags from the body yet.

"1:32 for the first half. Even if I slow down a little, say, 1:38 for the second half, I can still hit 3:10," I thought.

The math gave me quiet confidence. I knew the real test would come in the second half, as is always the case.

"Half job well done. Time to bring it home," I whispered to myself and got back to my movie.

Everything went smoothly until around the 34-kilometer mark.

That's when the lights started to flicker. My legs began to feel like they were dragging anchors. Holding the pace became a battle. My rhythm went off. My breath started hitching. The whole machine seemed to be falling apart, one gear at a time. I kept trying to push through, but the harder I tried, the more fragile I felt. It was that dreaded moment when the body stops negotiating and starts revolting.

Real life rarely follows the fairytale script we hope for. Keep going anyway.

"Cometh the moment, cometh the champion." I wish I could say that.

I wish I could say that I mustered all the courage to unleash the superhero in me. I wish I could say that I rose to the occasion to pull off what was seemingly impossible now. I wish I could say I found something deep within, an untapped reserve of grit or glory. I wish I could draw a fairytale finish.

But marathons aren't written like that. They don't follow Bollywood arcs. They're real, raw, and when they decide to humble you, they do it without mercy. It can be a totally unforgiving experience if things don't go your way. Things certainly didn't go my way that day.

As the watch crossed the 3:10 mark, I still had over 2 kilometers left. I wasn't even close. I had completely crumbled in the final stretch. I pulled the plug and walked the rest of the way, resigned, frustrated, and barely able to process what had gone wrong.

I finished in 3 hours and 25 minutes.

Just a year ago, I had proudly felt that I had reached the base camp of my running journey. Everything had felt within reach. But today, that same summit looked distant and jagged. The trail ahead now looked uncertain, steep, and littered with self-doubt.

I felt deflated—physically, mentally, emotionally, spiritually, and possibly even astrologically.

I sometimes wish life had a *Skip ad* button, a way to fast-forward the hard moments, to bypass the discomfort and struggle. A simple click, and the challenging phase would be behind me. But that's a luxury life doesn't offer. There's no easy escape, no shortcut. The only way out is through, no matter how uncomfortable it may feel.

Key Messages

i. **When life forces a reboot, listen.**
When we ignore the whispers, life sends a storm. Illness, setbacks, or forced pauses often arrive as nature's way of restoring balance. For a long time, I treated my body like a machine that could power through anything, until it couldn't. That stubborn cough wasn't just a medical condition; it was nature's way of holding up a mirror. It taught me that sometimes, slowing down is the most courageous thing you can do for your long-term journey.

ii. **Showing up is an act of faith.**
Even when I knew I couldn't run, I showed up. Not out of denial, but because showing up is my way of staying true to who I am. Life doesn't always offer the stage that you've prepared for, but sometimes, just standing in the wings is enough to receive something far more profound.

iii. Healing isn't linear, and neither is growth.
Progress rarely follows a straight path; it winds through detours we didn't plan. Just a year before, I was at the edge of the summit, within striking distance of the dream I had chased for years. Going by logic, time should have carried me closer. But here's the point—life loops, stalls, and sometimes even retreats to teach us things the peak never could. The hardest part isn't the distance; it's accepting that the map we drew doesn't match the terrain we're walking.

11

FALL SEVEN TIMES, STAND BACK UP EIGHT

The 100-day, 100-half-marathons commitment (just like that)

March 2019

ANOTHER year had gone by. As I sat down to reflect, it felt eerily similar to the one before it. Which, incidentally, had also felt suspiciously like the year before that. It was like living in a well-maintained time loop—the same inputs, discipline, and sacrifices. Yet, the Boston dream remained just that, a dream.

When I looked back at the past several years, what I saw was a life engineered around a singular pursuit: a disciplined diet, a strict sleep cycle, an impeccable workout regime, non-negotiable weekly mileage, and spreadsheets that would make a finance minister proud. Yet, despite all that effort, I wasn't any closer to qualifying for the Boston Marathon. A simmering frustration had started to bubble up. Clearly, I was missing something. The problem was that I had no idea what I needed to do.

In my quest for answers, I reached out to several running gurus across India. There were no silver bullets on offer. Just echoes of what I already knew, wrapped in marginally different packaging. Still, I kept digging. Weeks later, I finally stumbled upon two highly recommended running books: *Advanced Marathoning* by Pete Pfitzinger and Scott Douglas, and *Chi Running* by Danny Dreyer. I devoured them like a man who had just discovered carbs after years of keto diets. They were packed with insights, but one tip really stood out: the idea of gradually increasing mileage during training.

All these years, I had subscribed to the conventional wisdom that there exists a sweet spot for weekly mileage: Run too little and you're undertrained; run too much and you're injured. That belief hadn't changed. But now, I wondered if I'd been playing it too safe all along.

"How many kilometers should I run every week to improve as a runner?" I asked several runner friends, fishing for magic numbers. The most interesting reply came from a friend in the UK, Harry.

"As many as you can without getting injured," he replied, as if stating the bleeding obvious.

He hadn't said anything new, but it was the kind of obvious that only becomes profound when someone else says it.

"... And how do you know when you're about to get injured?" I asked, trying to dig deeper.

"I guess just keep increasing your mileage and you'll know when you do get injured."

He had said that in jest, but I took it in all seriousness. I decided to significantly increase my running volume.

As the universe would have it, around the same time, I came across an inspiring story about an Australian woman who was running long distances for 100 consecutive days to raise awareness about the global water crisis. Her story struck a chord with me, both as a runner and an environmentalist. I found myself wishing someone would do something like that in India, especially for air pollution, which had become an annual winter horror show in North India. No one could appreciate that better than I did, not after what had happened the previous year.

And then a wild idea started brewing.

"*Why don't I be that someone?*" I thought, almost startling myself.

That's the curious thing about life. It finds mysterious ways to nudge you toward what you're meant to do. On the one hand, my running research told me to run more. On the other hand, this meaningful cause was staring me in the face. Call it divine timing, coincidence, or just a perfectly timed identity crisis, but I didn't overthink it. I let the idea take over.

Within moments, the thought crystallized:

"I will run 100 half marathons in 100 consecutive days to spread awareness about air pollution."

I was very thrilled and a little nervous.

> *The path often reveals itself, not with fanfare, but with subtle signs. We just have to be willing to notice.*

No going back now

March 3, 2019, afternoon

It was a regular Sunday afternoon. Japneet and I were on our customary weekend coffee date, navigating the chaos of Gurugram traffic. My mind, though, was buzzing. As we pulled up at a red light, I dropped the bombshell.

"I'm planning to run 100 half marathons in 100 consecutive days."

Japneet took a moment to process this. You could almost hear the mental brakes screeching.

After a pause, she said, "I love how casually you said that. Like you're telling me what you had for lunch."

"Thank you," I replied with mock seriousness. "But what do you think of the idea?"

"If it were anyone else, I'd call it ridiculous. But with you, it feels weirdly normal. You live for this kind of madness, don't you?"

I smiled. She knew me well. More important, she had learned to embrace my madness with gentle humor and quiet support.

"So, when are you planning to start?

"Today."

She raised an eyebrow. "Running 100 half marathons in 100 days is a massive commitment. My two cents: Take a day to talk to your team at work and set expectations. Then, go for it."

"Hmm, okay. March 5 it is then." I did some quick mental math. "So, to be precise, it will be March 5 to June 12!"

The next morning, I walked into my mentor Prashant's cabin with the same casualness as I had while sharing a lunch-and-learn idea a few days back.

"Prashant, I'm planning to run 100 half marathons in 100 consecutive days to raise awareness about air pollution."

There was silence.

"What?!"

"Yes, you heard that right."

He looked stunned.

"Running 100 half marathons in 100 days sounds ... well, preposterous."

"Exactly," I grinned. "That's the appeal."

"Are you planning to take time off?"

"No. I'll work through the day. I'll run at night."

"What if you have to travel overseas?"

"I'll run overseas."

"What if you get injured?"

"I'll run with injuries."

He stared at me like he was unsure whether to laugh or call HR. Then, finally, he smiled.

"I can see you've made up your mind. As your well-wisher, I'm worried it might take a toll. But I also know that if you've decided to do it, you'll somehow pull it off. So, go for it."

Big decisions don't always need big debates. Sometimes, a quiet "yes" is enough.

"Thanks, Prashant."

Just as I was about to leave, he added, "It will be tougher than you think. More taxing than you can imagine. If at any stage you need anything, just ask. You have my support."

That same night, I sat down and finalized the structure for what I called The Right to Breathe Campaign. I'd always believed that air pollution was one of those problems everyone complains about, but no one really acts to solve the problem. Why? It could be due to apathy or ignorance. Either way, I wanted to shake people out of their indifference. And my weapon of choice? Running shoes.

The plan was simple: Use the daily runs to grab attention, and then use that attention window to convey high-impact messages about air pollution on social media.

I drafted my announcement post.

"100 Half Marathons in 100 Days: The Right to Breathe Campaign."

I read the message once, then again, and then one last time. I took a deep breath and clicked *Post*.

"There's no going back now," I whispered.

Getting introduced to fatigue on a first-name basis

March 5, 2019, Day 1 of the 100-day campaign

I stepped out for my run that evening, feeling like a sailor at the start of a long and uncertain voyage. I had no idea how the next 100 days would unfold. I wasn't even trying to imagine it.

"One day at a time," I told myself as I warmed up.

A few minutes later, I started jogging. Familiar route. Familiar pace. But something about it felt different. As I looped around the society track, I was met with high-fives and waves from fellow residents. A few smiles. A few nods. A few shouts of "Go for it!"

The campaign was officially underway. And so was the craziest journey of my life.

Life, as they say, is a great metaphor. If you look closely, it bears a striking resemblance to the many journeys we undertake—some grand, some modest. My 100-day running campaign was about to mirror its own little cycle of life.

For the first few days, the air around the campaign was electric. There was joy, excitement, and a whole lot of cheer. Wherever I ran, people would wave, clap, and cheer with the enthusiasm usually reserved for parade floats and cricket match victories. I would hear impromptu exclamations of "Bravo!", "Keep going!", "We're with you!" from casual walkers, gym-goers, security guards, kids on bicycles—you name it. For a few brief moments, I was the new celebrity on the block. Let's just say that I was the newborn baby of the neighborhood and everyone wanted to play peekaboo.

But like with all newborns, the novelty gradually wore off. About two weeks in, the cheers got quieter. The high-fives became more like polite nods. The head-turns turned into quick glances. People still appreciated what I was doing—at least I'd like to think so—but the sight of me lapping the same loop night after night had become part of the daily scenery. I had gone from being "Wow!" to "Oh, he's still running ..."

Don't rely too much on the applause at the start of any new journey—it fades away too quickly. Staying the course takes something far deeper.

It was only Day 15, and my body felt like it had been through a 15-month campaign. The fatigue was real. My legs felt heavier each evening, as though someone was secretly adding invisible ankle weights when I wasn't looking. The idea that I had to repeat this every single day for another 85 days was beginning to feel outright absurd. There were evenings when the thought of lacing up again felt physically and emotionally exhausting.

And yet, there was no backing out. I kept recalling Harry's voice in my head, "Keep increasing your mileage and you'll know your limit when you get injured." I was inching dangerously close to that limit.

What scared me more than the fatigue was the commitment I had made on social media. It wasn't just a personal goal anymore—it was a public declaration. There was no exit clause. No pause button. No *Ctrl+Z* to undo the decision. Rain, injury, long workdays, unpredictable travel—none of that mattered now. I had to run. Every. Single. Day.

Oddly enough, that rigidity helped. Often, confusion creeps in when there's room for negotiation, when your mind has the liberty to be reasonable. I had removed that luxury. There were no decisions to make, just actions to take.

On March 29, 2019, I hit my first major milestone: 25 half marathons in 25 days. I was elated. One quarter down.

"Just three more of these ridiculous quarters to go," I thought.

So, I chugged along, one run at a time.

The pounding on the body was relentless. I knew that if I wanted to survive the campaign, I had to double down on recovery. The basics became sacrosanct: Turmeric milk, ice packs, foam rolling, stretching, protein, and hydration became my full toolkit. I also stumbled upon a golden insight in one of the many articles I read during that time: "Sleep is the best recovery tool." It made perfect sense. If the body heals while you rest, then rest had to become non-negotiable.

So, I turned into a nap hunter.

Airports? Perfect. The seat near Gate 18 had my name on it. I exaggerate a bit, but only a bit. The Hop-on-Hop-off bus tour in Dublin? Great views of the city, also a great opportunity for a quick snooze. Waiting for my kid's school dismissal? A solid 17-minute power nap while the other parents scrolled on their phones.

I was shameless in my pursuit of sleep, and it worked. Those short bursts of recovery kept the engine running.

On some days, I ran like a well-oiled machine. On other days, I ran like a machine that badly needed servicing. But I kept going. Because that's what I had promised myself and the world.

Those 100 days turned me into a nap hunter

Too tired to go on, but too far ahead to turn back

April 23, 2019, Day 50 of the 100-day campaign

I kept dragging along, one run at a time.

Somewhere along the way, it felt like my body, mind and soul had settled into a state of equilibrium—a state of bliss where I felt no incremental pain or fatigue. I was still tired, still sore, still questioning all of my life choices—but not *more* than yesterday. Somehow, that felt like progress. It wasn't about recovery. It wasn't about resilience either. It was just normal. A new normal where my life collapsed into a predictable, oddly comforting cycle—lace up, warm up, run 21.1 km, stretch, recover, crash, repeat. It had stopped feeling like a campaign and started feeling like a job—except the job came with blisters, a warped toenail or two, and no pay.

On April 23, I reached another important milestone. It was time for the 50th half marathon. Already!

Like any self-respecting 1990s kid, I couldn't help but think about the timing of that milestone run. As I laced up that evening, I recalled the famous Desert Storm knocks Sachin had played in Sharjah on April 22 and 24 several years ago. The kid version of me had jumped around the living room like a sugar-crazed cricket fanatic. Now, the adult version was just trying to survive another half marathon in one piece. But for what it was worth, I had my own storm to ride out.

With the 50th run completed, I was now well and truly into the middle phase of the campaign.

Going back to the metaphor of life, the young kid had grown up to reach the midlife stage. I had come quite far from where I had started, but the end was nowhere in sight. I didn't have the energy to go any further, but returning was not an option either. I felt like a hapless soul lost in the deep woods. The grown-up was going through a midlife crisis.

To make matters worse, my fatigue had started to get creative. My left foot had swollen up as if it aspired to become a balloon. My regular shoes no longer fit, which left me with two options: Go barefoot or get creative with sizing. First, I tried wearing mismatched shoes—one regular-sized and the other clown-sized. I ran like a drunk flamingo for a day or two, but then I gave up and switched to barefoot running for a while. It was less elegant than it sounds.

Running on fumes and faith

May 11, 2019, Day 68 of the 100-day campaign

Some days punch you in the gut. Others throw the whole damn punchline at you. That evening was both. I was low on energy, hadn't had a great day at work, and just wanted to crawl into bed and not emerge until the campaign was over. I knew it was going to be a massive struggle to finish the run that day. At around 9 p.m., I reached the start line. I just wanted to be done with it. But such is the nature of long-distance running that you cannot just be done with it. I had to navigate a painful two hours ahead to just get done for the day.

I stood at my usual starting point, staring at my foot. It looked pitiable—puffy and discolored—the kind of foot that wouldn't look out of place in a medical journal under "Case study: what not to do." I was supposed to do a warm-up, but what was the point? The whole idea of a warm-up is to avoid injury. I had already moved far beyond that stage. Injury wasn't a risk; it was now a roommate.

Without thinking too much about it, I hit *Start* on the watch and shuffled forward. My body protested, my feet ached, and my mind did its usual trick of listing all the better things I could be doing with my evening. But the rhythm returned eventually. It always did. I wasn't sure if that was resilience or just muscle memory doing its job while the rest of me quietly fell apart.

Either way, Day 68 was underway.

In my most personal moments during the run, I often found myself flirting with the idea of aborting the campaign and returning to normal life—the kind where your feet don't swell into balloons and your shoes don't need to be sourced from two different size racks. This thought typically surfaced as a familiar argument within me. Some days it was a mild debate; on others, it had the intensity of a full-blown courtroom drama.

As I hobbled along with my mismatched feet that evening, I could sense the usual suspects gearing up for another internal face-off.

me: *"Enough of this drama now."*

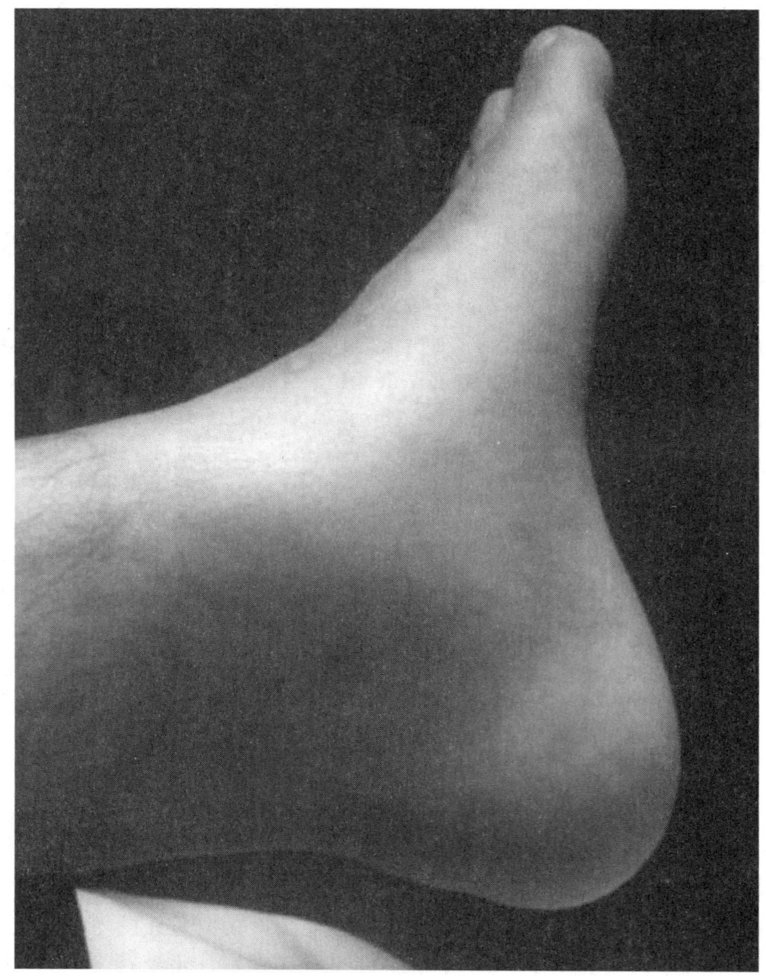

My left foot on the 68th day of the 100-day campaign

No response.

me: *"Are you listening to what I am saying?"*

ME: *"Yes, I am."*

me: *"Goddamn it, then say something."*

ME: *"I didn't come this far to only come this far. There is no going back now. I have to complete it."*

me: *"That won't happen anyway. Look at your feet. You think you can go on running half marathons like this for the next 32 days?"*

ME: *"I don't know."*

me: *"Of course you do. It's a matter of time before this stupid campaign of yours crumbles under its own weight."*

No response.

me: *"The decision is yours. Either you do it sanely, gracefully accepting the inevitable, or have it forcefully thrust upon you with injuries taking a toll."*

No response.

me: *"You are worried about how you will face people if you abort it midway, isn't it?"*

ME: *"No."*

me: *"Then, what is it?"*

ME: *"I am worried about how I will face myself."*

There was no argument thereafter. I continued with my awkward gait. Given the uneven landing pattern, my feet produced a somewhat different music that night: "thud thatch thud thatch thud thatch ..."

At around 11:15 p.m., I finished the 68th half marathon in as many days.

Courage isn't about facing others; it's about confronting the reflection within.

Lights, Camera ... Run!

I had now managed to survive the insanity for over 75 days. The last quarter of the campaign was here, and it was starting to feel a little surreal. The campaign had also begun to gain visibility. I was starting to receive calls from friends and well-wishers, each with their own version of encouragement, but none more memorable than my old college friend, Simon Jacob.

Simon and I had studied together at IIM Kozhikode and graduated in 2007. We were good friends back in the day, but like so many college friendships, life had drifted us apart. It had been nearly 12 years since we last spoke.

Then, one evening, I received a call from an unknown number.

"Am I speaking to Sundy?" said a voice that felt oddly familiar.

I knew it was some old college friend. Nobody referred to me by that name anymore.

"Yes, who's this?"

"Simon."

"Holy cow, Simon! How are you? Where have you been?"

"Doesn't matter. What matters is you just finished your 77th half marathon!"

"Have you been following the campaign?"

"Of course, I am following it. We all are. Clearly, you haven't changed since college."

"In what sense?" I asked curiously.

"You are as insane today as you were back in the day!" he said, in a tone that mixed concern and pride.

His voice underpinned a sense of pride. He continued, "Listen, what you're doing requires incredible effort. More people need to know about it—about the message behind your madness."

"You have something in mind?"

"Yes, I've spoken to a client of mine. They're keen to make a short video about your campaign. We'll release it on June 5, World Environment Day."

"This is amazing! What do I need to do?"

"You'll need to find time for a few video shoots—running at various locations—and record a voiceover. Are you up for it?"

"Yes, Sir! Totally game. Thank you so much!"

Running had already brought so much joy and surprise into my life, and now it was offering yet another first—an on-camera debut. I was buzzing with excitement.

Within a week, we began shooting. The plan was to stitch together a short film showing me running across various landscapes—village roads, flyovers, highways, riverbanks—while my voice narrated the essence of the campaign. The vibe was intentionally emotional. We wanted to create something that would inspire people to think and act differently about air pollution.

Of course, this campaign shoot was in addition to the daily half marathons I still had to complete. It added to the fatigue, no doubt, but the experience made it worthwhile. I gained deep appreciation for an industry I had once casually dismissed as just "lights, camera, action." I found out that shooting was a lot more than just pressing *Record* and adding some jazz. There's planning, timing, angles, and most surprisingly, redoing the same scene over and over just to get it right. I may not have learned to act, but I definitely learned to respect the craft.

By the time I crossed Day 85, I could feel the finish line calling. The child had grown into an adult, the adult had faced his midlife crisis, and now, this cranky old runner was preparing for retirement.

The reverse countdown had officially begun.

The run that broke me, well, almost

May 31, 2019, Day 88 of the 100-day campaign

For a campaign as physically demanding as this one, things had gone suspiciously smoothly until that point. Sure, I was running on fumes—physically drained, teetering on the edge, practically in a flirtatious long-distance relationship with injury—but that was something I expected from the moment I signed up for it. Barring those obvious challenges, there had been no surprises along the way. That situation changed on Day 88.

I was in Mumbai on a work trip and got free by around 8 p.m. The plan was to get to the hotel, freshen up, and hit the road. But for some reason, I felt unusually anxious. I had this gnawing feeling that something wasn't quite right. I checked myself—shoes, socks, watch, energy gel, and water bottle were all in place. Yet, something was off. I've never really bought into the whole sixth-sense mumbo-jumbo, but if such a thing does exist, it was right there, and it was telling me that I would not get through the run that night.

I ignored it and headed out. The run started fine, and I eventually managed to shake off that irksome vibe. I had just crossed the 14-kilometer mark when I heard a beep from my watch.

Low Battery.

My heart sank. Amid the work calls, travel shuffle, and the mental circus of the day, I had forgotten to charge my watch. Big mistake. I had never forgotten before, not during the campaign, not even in regular life. This was a first, and not the kind you write home about.

Still, the optimist in me believed my watch had at least seven more kilometers in it. I picked up the pace, hoping to outrun both exhaustion and technology. At around the 18th kilometer, two more beeps rang out. I hesitated before checking the screen.

Battery critically low.

It was referring to the watch's battery, but it was true for me too.

"No, no, no, please don't give up on me tonight. I need you to stay with me for 15 more minutes, please," I pleaded, staring helplessly at the watch, running a tad faster.

Just before the 19-kilometer mark, I heard the final beep for that night. I looked at the screen. There was no message. The battery had run out completely. It was the blank black screen I was dreading. No more beeps or goodbyes—just ... silence. My faithful companion for 88 days had quit on me without ceremony.

Any step thereafter would not be recorded, so technically, the run would not qualify as a half marathon. I kept running though. I'm still not sure why. Maybe I hoped the watch would miraculously reboot. Maybe I was too numb to process what had just happened. After a few hundred meters, my inner voice returned.

me: *"The watch is dead. Why are you still running?"*

No reply from "ME."

me: *"Idiot! Have you lost it completely? Just stop. Now."*

In all my "me" versus "ME" conversations (or should I say, altercations), that was probably the only time when "ME" had no reply.

I gradually slowed down, confused and disoriented. I looked around. There was dead silence all around, silence that seemed deafening. I wandered over to a bench and sat down helplessly. I didn't even know where I was in the city. The 88th day had ended. My run count stood frozen at 87. I thought that was the end of the campaign.

I hate to admit it, but that was the one moment in the campaign when I cried.

I am not sure how long I sat there. I have no memory of what I thought, or even if I thought anything. It was a brain fog. I am not sure how the fog eventually cleared or how long it took. But what I do remember is the thought that I eventually got up with.

"I am one run short. To make up for it, I need to run 13 half marathons in the next 12 days."

On reaching the hotel room, I made the entry in my daily journal:

"88 days complete; 87 half marathons complete."

It took every ounce of willpower to scribble those words, maybe even more than it takes to run a half marathon.

The silence after a failure can be deafening, but that's where resilience is born.

Push until something happens

June 6, 2019, Day 94 of the 100-day campaign

I was on the 94th day of the campaign. That was the day I had reserved to knock off two half marathons, making up for the backlog from the night my watch had pulled the plug on me. At around 12:45 a.m., I stepped out.

P.U.S.H: Push Until Something Happens

I'd once seen this acronym plastered outside a sports academy. What intrigued me most was how the acronym featured its own word in the expansion, almost lending it a recursive, eternal quality: PUSH until something happens, until something happens, until something happens …

You could loop that for eternity, which, coincidentally, is also how long I felt I'd been running.

The beauty of the message lay in its simplicity. If you're up to something, just keep pushing. Don't worry about things outside your control. Focus on what's within your reach—P.U.S.H.

Preparing to start the run, I found myself thinking about this acronym. I am not sure where and how I landed on that thought. If you think about it, and I did think about it, it's fascinating how the human mind traverses across space and time to dig out strange artefacts. I tried to replay the chain of thoughts in my mind to discover how I landed on that acronym, but I got no answer. A moment ago, I was thinking about something completely unrelated, and suddenly, this acronym buoyed up to the top of my conscious mind.

Nonetheless, I did intend to PUSH that day, push as hard as I could against the monstrous task of running two back-to-back half marathons after running half marathons for the previous 93 days.

I have very limited memory of that run. I remember making a conscious effort to stay thought-free as much as possible. I kept putting one foot ahead of the other, without worrying about how far I had come or how far I needed to go. What I also remember is that toward the second half of the run, the acronym I had been thinking about at the start of the race had become a melodious mantra that I was constantly chanting. I settled into a nice little rhythm, with the sound of my feet syncing with the infinite expansion of the acronym that I was continuously murmuring: "Tap, tap, tap … tap, tap, tap … tap, tap, tap … until something happens … until something happens… until something happens …"

I completed the run around 3:15 a.m. I took a quick nap (read: passed out) and came back later that morning to finish the second half marathon for the day. When the sun went down, my journal read:

"94 days complete. 94 half marathons complete."

I was both relieved and happy, slightly more relieved than happy.

> *One more step. That's all progress ever asks for. At the end of the day, every finish line in life comes down to a string of "one more step" moments.*

A century of showing up

June 12, 2019, Day 100 of the 100-day campaign

Battling fatigue and exhaustion, I reached the 99th day of the campaign. I was just one day away from what would become one of my most cherished memories.

As I lay in bed that night, I couldn't get my mind away from the final run that awaited me the next day. I reflected upon the three months that had gone by. I had pushed myself beyond what I ever thought I was capable of. I had experienced all types of runs through those three months: joyful, painful, thoughtful, reflective, energetic, lethargic. Life had been centered on the half marathon for that day, and one day at a time was the guiding principle. All of that would now culminate in that one final run, the 100th run. There was a sense of thrill and gratitude.

Deep within, there was also a sense of anxiety. As much as I was excited about the final run, I was also worried about the day after. It was hard to imagine what the day would feel like without having to think about a half marathon. It was not that I'd been madly enjoying running a half marathon every day. If anything, I had often questioned my decision to sign up for it. But now that it was coming to an end, it felt like the time had come to bid adieu to a cherished possession, something that belonged *only* to me, something that I had started secretly loving despite all its shortcomings.

The next morning, just before leaving for work, I made a simple one-line social media post:

"June 12, 2019. 100th half marathon in 100 days at 8 p.m. at The Retreat Society Complex. Can't wait!"

I kept the workday light. I wanted to preserve every ounce of energy for that final run. Later in the evening, I reached the starting point early, hydration bottles in hand, just in case someone showed up to run with me.

As I did my warm-up drills, I looked around. I was sad to see that no one had shown up, not a single soul.

"So much for 100 consecutive half marathons for a cause!" I chuckled, smirking at myself as I started jogging around the loop.

But just as I completed the first round, I saw a lone figure standing nearby, watching me closely. As I passed him, he raised both hands and bowed.

I paused, taken aback.

"Thank you, my friend, for coming over. It means a lot," I said, my voice cracking slightly.

With every lap I ran after that, more people began to gather. One, then two, then ten. Half an hour in, runners began joining me, taking turns, matching strides. There wasn't a single moment in the remainder of that final run when I was running alone.

And then it happened.

I crossed the imaginary finish line. The 100th run was complete.

I stood there amidst friends—some old, some brand new—smiling, soaked, and stunned. Gratitude swelled within me. And just then, a little voice rang out from a distance. I turned to see Ekam beaming as he announced proudly to a group of kids, "That's my Dad!"

Celebrating the successful completion of the 100-day-100-half-marathon campaign with friends

It was a tiny sentence. But it knocked the wind out of me. That one sentence made the entire journey—the sweat, the soreness, the solitude—completely worth the effort.

That night, as I sat quietly at home, replaying the moment in my head, I finally understood the wisdom of an overused quote I'd always brushed off:

"Life is not measured by the number of breaths we take, but by the moments that take our breath away."

That night, I certainly had a brief little moment that took my breath away.

I had run 2,110 kilometers for over 200 hours, spread over 10 cities across 100 days to have earned that *brief moment.*

Life's true measure lies in the moments that pause everything else.

S.T.E.P: A Runner's Perseverance Mantra

Some people are good at persevering until they get what they want, while others tend to quit midway through a pursuit. Ever wondered what differentiates them?

It's the way their minds operate every time there is a desire to quit. Those who persevere recognize that the real battle is not in the long path ahead, but in the moment when they consider quitting. They are able to shift their attention away from the long journey ahead to the all-important one step that truly matters in the moment: the next one.

They think: **Just One More S.T.E.P.**

S.T.E.P: A Runner's Perseverance Mantra

S: Shift the horizon.	• Converge all your attention to your immediate vicinity, both in space and time. • As counterintuitive as it may sound, think small—as small as one step.
T: Tweak the definition of success.	• Don't obsess over the gigantic end milestone. • Redefine what success means to you. In the moment of doubt, not stopping itself is a success.
E: Enjoy small wins along the way.	• With the tweaked definition of success, every step becomes a success. • Success walks with you rather than feeling miles away. • Feel good about these minor victories. Let these small successes energize you.
P: Put one foot forward.	• You don't need to see the whole path. • Just take the next step, in good faith. And then the next. And then one more.

An illustration of how I used this mantra: During the 100-days-100-half-marathons effort, there were several days when I woke up flirting with the idea of quitting midway. My legs used to be tired. My motivation had quietly checked out. On each of those occasions, I used to tell myself: "Maybe just wear the shoes." Then, "Maybe just walk to the gate." By the time I hit the first kilometer, something clicked. The rhythm returned.

Through those days, I learned an important lesson. I never needed to feel ready for 21.1 kilometers. I just needed to be willing to take one more step. The mantra has stayed with me ever since:

"At any point in a journey, you don't need the ammunition to go all the way—you need just enough to take the next step."

Key Messages

i. **Sometimes, the most irrational decisions lead to the most meaningful outcomes.**
Some goals sound outrageous—because they are. And that's their beauty. The mind may protest, the world may scoff, but if your heart says "yes," listen to it. Say it out loud. Declare it. Then begin. One quiet step at a time. In chasing the illogical, you often find your most honest self. Had I tried to be logical, I would have never signed up for 100 half marathons, but I am glad I chose to be illogical, for it gave me joy that no logic ever could.

ii. **PUSH, until something happens.**
Mantras don't have to be profound to be powerful. Sometimes the simplest ones, repeated through exhaustion, pain, and disorientation, hold the potential to become life anchors. Be like a woodpecker, a small bird with its delicate beak searching for food inside a tree trunk. It knows one hit won't do it. Ten hits won't do it. But it keeps going, hit after hit, knock after knock, until the bark yields, until something happens! That's persistence. That's focus. That's how goals are achieved.

iii. **Rest if you must, but do not quit.**
In life, as in long-distance running, what matters is the spirit to move forward despite all hardships. As long as you can gather the courage to put one foot ahead of the other, you have the license to thump your chest and proudly shout, "Game on!"

12

YOU ARE STRONGER THAN YOU THINK

When the world came to a halt

THE 100-day half-marathon streak was a remarkable journey of self-discovery.

During those runs, I often found myself pondering some of life's most difficult and un-Googleable questions: "Who am I? Why am I here? Where am I headed? What is my purpose? What happens if I vanish? What are my values? Why are those values good? Are they even *mine*, or do I just rent them for social occasions? Am I a good person?" And sometimes, I would even have questions about the questions: "Why do these questions matter? Should they matter?"

I never really found answers. I still haven't. But interestingly, I noticed a trend: These philosophical ambushes usually arrived during times of extreme stress.

Stress, physical stress to be precise, was one thing that I had in rich abundance in those days. It was taking a toll on my body day after day, but my body declined all the sane suggestions that my mind was providing. That caused my mind to start its own revolt, almost as a way of telling the body, "You are doing more than your fair share of nonsense, so how can I stay far behind?" Those questions were a way of the mind competing with the body to attain an elevated nonsense index, if there is a measurement like that.

In normal circumstances, I would never have done something like my 100-day campaign. The whole idea was an aberration, a disturbance that erupted in my mind one fine day and took me along. Not much thought went into it. It was just a turbulent wave that was meant to be, and it happened. It had now been around six months since the campaign ended. The euphoria associated with the campaign had died long ago. Most people, other than my nearest and dearest ones, had forgotten about it. But for me, the aftermath of the campaign continued for much longer.

In some ways, the campaign changed me forever. I was never the same person after getting over those 100 days. It was like a high-amplitude shock wave that rendered me significantly moderated forever. Upside and downside fences had been placed on the intensity with which I could feel any emotion. Nothing could excite, sadden, gratify, depress, or concern me to the magnitude of the pre-campaign days. I was not oblivious to those changes either. I noticed them most in social situations. While people laughed, cheered, debated, or fretted, I often found myself stepping back, quietly observing *myself*, like I was auditioning for the role of "Detached Guy in Group Settings."

While I was busy coping with my own inconsequential turbulence, there was a gigantic wave of turbulence that was getting ready to wreak havoc across the world: the COVID-19 virus.

When I first heard about it, I gave a big, wide, hippo-style yawn. I brazenly dismissed it as a desperate media attempt to lift TRPs. But within days, things started to get bad, really bad. It didn't take long to recognize that the menace was real. By mid-March in 2020, India imposed its first nationwide lockdown in an attempt to check the spread of the contagious virus. The nation came to a halt.

In the early days of the pandemic, the talk used to be, "I know someone who has a friend who has a COVID-positive case in their extended family." It soon shifted to, "I know someone who has a positive case in their family," and before anyone knew, the conversation had become, "Someone in my family has contracted COVID-19." It was like a big, wide, spherical envelope of fear and death that was rapidly descending on us. Everyone was waking up to the harsh reality that sooner or later, their turn would come.

Such was the magnitude of the calamity that everything else started feeling inconsequential in comparison. Everything stopped. No get-togethers, no getting out of the house, nothing. With the exception of select emergency services, everything came to a halt. Running, of course, wasn't on the government's list of essential services. By the end of April, every race I'd signed up for was either cancelled or indefinitely postponed. At an individual level, I was disappointed. But in the larger context, being alive and healthy had become the new luxury item. Not getting a chance to take a stab at my BQ dream was no big deal.

Even the strongest routines crumble in the face of uncertainty—and that's okay.

Several weeks rolled by. The world was experimenting with new ways to get back into some kind of motion. It couldn't have stayed in a state of permanent halt forever. Online schooling became the new normal. Working from home became synonymous with pajama-collar meetings. The rules of social gatherings changed every week, and the world collectively Googled, "What is quarantine fatigue?"

We runners were no exception. We were left fidgeting at home, trying to create meaning out of push-ups and burpees. Some brave souls took to running with masks, sneaking out at dawn like masked vigilantes. I wasn't quite there yet. It's not that I hadn't thought about it. But I settled for indoor routines that were more tragic than athletic: running inside the room while dodging chairs or on-the-spot jogging that moved neither body nor soul. These were makeshift solutions at best, and none of them could replicate the therapy of open-road running. I felt like a tightly coiled spring, storing more tension with every passing day.

That spring finally uncoiled around mid-August.

The spring-loaded toy decides to uncoil

August 21, 2020

It was a typical Friday evening. I sat at my desk, staring blankly at the screen, not really thinking—just existing. I hadn't yet wrapped up my work and still had a few emails to send before closing for the day. A part of me was beginning to think about the plan for the weekend ahead. With COVID restrictions, there weren't too many options to choose from anyway. After thinking about it for a while, I comfortably reclined in my chair and let out the widest yawn of the day, one that could rival any animal's in a wildlife documentary. After fidgeting in the chair for a few moments, I walked out to the balcony and leaned over the parapet. The street below was empty, and so was my motivation. In the good old pre-COVID days, this would've been my tempo run hour.

Just then, casually, almost innocently, a thought crossed my mind.

"What if I go out for a short run tonight?"

It was a simple, harmless thought, one that didn't merit any serious attention. But once that door cracked open, a hundred internal voices barged in.

"It's been over six months since you stepped out."

"You have been a good, responsible citizen, diligently following social-distancing norms."

"Stepping out just once for a run won't hurt."

"There is no risk of you contracting the virus because there is hardly anyone on the road."

Please, think about it."

I tried to resist, but the voices were louder than logic. Within minutes, I had my sneakers laced, and just like that, I was on the road again.

I felt like a spring-loaded toy from childhood, the kind you wind up and let loose. The more tightly it is wound, the farther and faster it goes. If there ever was an incarnation of those toys, it was right there on the road that evening, merrily running around the society complex, unwinding all the pent-up energy. The more I ran, the more I wanted to run.

Around 30 minutes in, another thought slipped in, uninvited of course.

"What if I run 100 kilometers tonight?"

I wondered where that random idea came from. I had never consciously thought about doing it. Yet, it carried an irresistible appeal and felt like an idea worth building upon. Within moments, my trusted companions, "me" and "ME," convened an emergency meeting.

Random thoughts are often whispers from within. What may feel like a fleeting idea could be your inner compass calling. Honor it before it fades.

me: *"Don't be stupid. You're just six kilometers into a run. You cannot randomly decide to run 100 kilometers through the night."*

ME: *"Why not?"*

me: *"Because it requires diligent planning!"*

ME: *"Like?"*

me: *"Like you will need proper hydration if you must run through the night."*

ME: *"If I don't return home for some time, Japneet will come out to check on me. I will request her to keep some water bottles and energy drinks near the society gate. It's a circular loop anyway, so that should do the job. Happy?"*

me: *"Given the humidity, you will sweat like crazy. You will need at least 10 T-shirts to run through the night."*

ME: *"Don't worry, I will just take this one off, so I will need none."*

me: *"What about your shoes? Soon, your shoes and socks will be soaked in sweat, then it's a matter of time before you get blisters."*

ME: *"Stop giving such useless excuses. I am running on the society loop. I can always take a break and step into new shoes if and when I need to."*

me: *"Since you had not planned for this run, you didn't charge your GPS watch. The charge will run out shortly. How will you measure distance then? I don't need to tell you how it feels when the battery gives up on you. Remember Day 88?"*

That seemed like the only valid argument "me" had offered. It needed a bit of thought.

ME: *"So, here is the plan: As soon as I see Japneet in the balcony, I will request her to put the other watch for charging. I will run with this one until it lasts and then switch to the other one, putting this one for charging. This is exactly the day for which I bought two watches."*

Before "me" could throw any further objections, I saw Japneet waving at me from our first-floor balcony. I took a slight detour to move closer to the balcony.

"I am feeling hungry. Should I wait for dinner?" she asked.

"Please go ahead. I will take some more time, but do wait for me for breakfast," I shouted back.

She blinked, "What are you up to now?"

"Hundred kilometers."

"What!"

"Hundred kilometers," I repeated.

"I heard the first time. It was an exclamation, not a question," she replied with a gentle nod and an amused smile. She took a few moments to let it sink in and then asked, "Need some help?"

"Yes, please see me at the society gate in some time," I shouted back and moved on.

A few minutes later, I met Japneet at the gate and explained everything I needed: water, energy drinks, shoe changes, a charged watch, and whatever else that came to mind in that rather short planning window I had allowed myself for the all-nighter.

So began the night run of a lifetime.

A hundred kilometers of solitude

I felt a thrill creep in, the kind I hadn't felt since Day 1 of my 100-days-100-half-marathons campaign. I had missed that excitement of venturing into unknown territory so much.

I jogged along, soaking up every bit of natural stimulus we runners secretly romanticize. The earthy scent, rustling breeze, birds chirping their unsolicited playlist, the moon sliding into its prime-time slot .... Even the air felt uncharacteristically fresh, like it had just been laundered—the perks of a global economic nap. Just being out on the road felt like stepping into a beautifully orchestrated illusion. Not long ago, this was my routine. But in the post-COVID world, it felt like fine dining, and I was bingeing on it.

We often overlook life's everyday miracles until a forced pause makes us see how extraordinary the ordinary really is.

I had been running for close to five hours when I casually glanced at my watch to check how far I had come. I blinked. I'd already crossed the full marathon distance. Odd. I wasn't feeling the usual post-marathon corpse vibes. Partly, it was because of the pace. I was running significantly slower than at any official event. But I suspect there was more to it, something about the way our crafty minds operate. In a marathon, the brain "knows" it needs to power through 42 kilometers, so it carefully schedules body complaints across the route. But tonight? It "knew" I was gunning for 100 kilometers. Complaining this early would've been premature and pointless. So, it merrily rolled with it, drama-free.

It was 1:30 a.m. I was still enjoying the experience, but the vibe had shifted. The ambience around me had changed significantly. The odd late-night walkers had sneaked away. The melodious chirping of birds had given way to shrill insect sounds. I couldn't spot any dogs on the street either; they too had probably gone to sleep. All I could see was a clear, cloudless sky with a beautiful moon proudly shining on that dark night. There was an eerie silence. The only human exposure I had was in the form of the society guard who curiously stared at me every time I crossed the gate. He was probably trying to make sense of what I was up to, or maybe he was hoping for me to end the run so he could take a nap too. I was enjoying his confused expressions. For a short while through that night, I remember looking forward to watching his expressions at the end of each round. On that long night, one would do anything to keep the mind engaged.

It was now close to 3 a.m. The body had moved past "tired" into "violently opposed." It was feeling physically drained, even "abused." I could sense that it was a matter of time before it would summon me, "Enough! Time to go back home."

I wondered if I had ever experienced that kind of fatigue in my life. But just as the mental white flag was ready to rise, a voice echoed from deep within, *"You have a short memory! Once upon a time, you ran 100 half marathons in 100 days, and ...."*

I didn't need my mind to complete the thought. A smile cracked through my fatigue. That was the spark I needed. I pushed on.

Thud, thud, thud, thud ...

There's something oddly poetic about the sound of footsteps in the dark. To me, it signifies, *"Just the man and his will to survive ...."*

I dragged along for another hour, drenched in sweat. My feet were feeling sore with all the pounding. I was running as slow as I could for it to still qualify as running, but my breath was labored. I desperately needed to change my clothes. But I've always felt that true fatigue doesn't hit during a run—it waits until you stop, like a tax audit. It's almost like during the run, the momentum carries you along, but once you halt, the whole system has to be started all over again. I was scared that if I went home, I wouldn't be able to come back. By around

4 a.m., however, I had no option but to take that chance. I vowed to come back and shuffled home.

At home, I went to the washroom and quickly undressed. First the T-shirt, then the shorts, then the shoes. I paused before taking off my socks. I was expecting an unpleasant sight, one that could have provided a strong reason for not going back. I grudgingly took them off and was not at all surprised at what I saw. There were six blisters, all in varying stages of rebellion—some large, some small, some that had already burst, others that were waiting to burst. I still had about 30 kilometers to go, and that sight was not helping my cause. I rapidly wiped myself with a fresh towel and slipped into fresh running gear.

As I struggled to put on the socks, an internal debate flared up.

me: *"There's a fine line between bravery and stupidity."*

ME: *"Right. This is bravery. Look at the feet—it takes guts to even think about continuing."*

me: *"That's exactly my point. Look at the feet. It is insane to think you can pull off 30 kilometers in this state."*

No reply.

me: *"Any comments?"*

ME: *"Maybe you are right."*

me: *"Good, so you are not going back?"*

ME: *"That's not what I said. I said you may be right."*

me: *"Be definite. Going or not going?"*

ME: *"If I go back, I may still not complete the run, but if I don't go back, I will certainly NOT complete it."*

Before "me" could build a stronger case, "ME" decisively stepped in.

ME: *"I am going back. We'll take it from there. See you on the track, buddy."*

I was back outside by 4:30 a.m. Restarting was awful, like trying to wake up a cranky teenager. My calves were cramped, and hamstrings were grumpy. But all I needed to do now was move forward. Just one foot, then the next. I resumed.

As I passed the society gate, I saw the guard again. His expression had changed through the night. It had shifted from confusion to boredom. Yes, he was definitely bored of me. He was probably waiting for the early-morning walkers to show up as much as I was.

About an hour later, a few early-morning walkers showed up. I knew some of them would greet me, as they always did. But I didn't have the strength to reciprocate. I knew it might look rude, but with my fast-depleting reserves, I focused all my attention on the next step ahead. That is not to say that I wasn't relieved to see them. Yes, I was waiting for them, for I knew there was every chance that I would faint, and I didn't want to lie there on the road unattended.

I continued to look down and chug along. I noticed myself humming the same old acronym that had helped me about a year back: P.U.S.H; thud, thatch, thud … thud, thatch, thud … thud, thatch, thud … until something happens … until something happens … until something happens …

I kept breathing in and breathing out, putting one foot ahead of the other as if my life depended on it. In a strange way, my life did depend on it, because knowing myself, I would never have allowed myself to go back without breaking the 100-kilometer barrier.

Sometimes, the fiercest weapon you have is persistence—one foot ahead of the other. Repeat.

"I saw you running from my window late last night, and I see you are running in the morning too. How much did you sleep?" I heard someone asking curiously.

"I will sleep when I am done running," I replied. I didn't bother checking who it was.

"What do you mean?"

"I mean what I said. I will sleep when I am done, seven more to go for hundred," I chugged along, staring intimidatingly at the ground, thinking about the famous lines from a poem by Robert Frost.

"The woods are lovely, dark and deep,
But I have promises to keep,
And miles to go before I sleep."

Interesting news has a way of spreading out. Someone running through the night trying to finish 100 kilometers was certainly interesting enough for sane people. Before I knew, all of the morning walkers knew what I was up to. I could sense it in the way they were staring at me, some with bewilderment, others with sympathy for my dilapidated condition.

I kept chugging along, ever so slowly, one foot ahead of the other.

I had been running for close to 11 hours. That's a significant amount of time to be doing something uninterrupted. I tried to recall if I had ever done something, anything, for that long at a stretch. Nothing came to mind. In my conscious memory, I couldn't recall even sleeping for that long at a stretch. But here I was, swinging my arms back and forth, trying to catch my dead-tired body from falling over every time my wobbly foot landed ahead of the other. I still had about seven kilometers to go.

"Almost there," I whispered to myself.

I vaguely remember that in the last few kilometers, I had this fearful sensation of losing my cognitive and sensory faculties. A brain fog inhibited my ability to think clearly. I was struggling with basic mental calculations. After completing the 97th kilometer, I recall struggling to calculate how many more kilometers I had to cover. Computing the difference between 100 and 97 suddenly felt like a gigantic task, like advanced calculus. The brain was probably not getting enough oxygen to perform basic functions. I couldn't feel anything either. I had been robotically repeating the same pattern of body movements through the night, but I did not think it would literally reduce me to a robot with respect to my ability to feel anything. I had an insatiable desire to gulp water, yet a strange gut feeling told me that I would vomit if I consumed even a sip. Every single body part was crying with pain, yet a strange sensation required me not to endure that pain anymore. Pain was a mere sensation that did not trouble me any longer. I felt like a mish-mash of confused organs loosely packed inside organic packaging material called skin.

Just before I finished the 100-kilometer journey, I recall I was no longer battling pain or fatigue. I felt like I had been elevated into a different world, where pain and fatigue didn't feel the same as they do in the real world. I was struggling with an identity crisis, feeling like a stranger to myself. I didn't know who I was, what I wanted, or what I had been doing all night. It was surreal, detached.

Eventually, I crossed the 100-kilometer mark. I did not stop though. I wasn't sure if that was the right thing to do. I helplessly looked within, turning to "me" and "ME" to get some guidance.

In a rare moment, they both spoke the same words.

me: *"You should stop now."*

ME: *"Yes, you can stop now."*

Those two voices saying the same thing didn't feel right either. If anything, it added to the confusion.

Normally "me," the wiser voice, would caution me, hold me back. And "ME" would fight back, resist, urge me to push forward. Yet here they were, saying the same thing. It felt wrong. The certainty in their voices unsettled me, as if I had no choice.

Despite the unsettling feeling, I stopped.

I slowly limped my way to the society lawn nearby. I crashed on the grass and lay there beneath the wide-open blue sky. There was sweat, exhaustion, fatigue, confusion, and much more. I closed my eyes and gradually allowed a myriad of conflicting feelings to sink in. What is more, I seemed to have reached a higher state where none of those feelings could bother me.

> *We can't always control what we feel, but we can choose how deeply we let it affect us.*

What remained wasn't triumph or loss; it was simply a moment of stillness, a release of all that had been fought.

I was at peace.

A few people gathered around me, probably thinking I was dead, but I didn't care. I was alive. And that was enough. I rose slowly, the world feeling quieter somehow, my mind clearer.

Smiling, I made my way back home with a sense of peace I hadn't anticipated.

Key Messages

i. **You don't need ideal conditions, just the intent to begin.**

When I decided to run through the night, there was no race bib, no cheering crowd, not even proper gear or preparation. But that night, the intent to run 100 kilometers was so clear, so deeply rooted, that it overpowered every excuse. And once that intent took the first step, the rest of me followed.

ii. **The body is far more capable than what the mind makes it believe.**

When exhaustion sets in, the first to raise its hand is never the body. It's the voice in the head that wants comfort and predictability. But I've learned that the line between "I can't" and "I can" is mostly mental. When you stop negotiating with discomfort and keep moving, step by step, the magic happens. Our ceilings are rarely structural; they're psychological.

iii. **The most profound moments often arrive quietly. Embrace them.**

Finishing that 100-kilometer run didn't feel like crossing a finish line. It felt like dissolving into something I didn't fully understand: fatigue, confusion, stillness, surrender. There was no euphoria, only a quiet truth: I had touched something elemental within me. Not all wins look like glory. Some arrive softly, not to validate you, but to introduce you to yourself.

13

ALL IT TAKES IS *ALL* YOU'VE GOT

The dream returns, quietly

February 2022

WE human beings are judgmental by nature. Consciously or unconsciously, we are always judging others around us—their beliefs, actions, fears, aspirations, just about everything. We seem to have an opinion on everyone we interact with. We all do it to some degree, some more than others. I, for one, have been proudly doing it for nearly four decades. If there was an Olympic event for silently analyzing the world around me with mildly raised eyebrows, I'd at least make it to the finals.

When you do something for that long, you ought to become really good at it. Yes, logically speaking, I should have mastered the art of understanding people by now, especially those close to me. Yet, it feels bizarre that for the longest time, I have not understood the one person I've been stuck with for every waking, sleeping, and running moment of my life—myself.

Sometimes, it takes a shock to break the trance. The first jolt for me came during the 100-day-100-half-marathons challenge. That endeavor nudged a few loose cobwebs upstairs. Suddenly, I was thinking thoughts I'd never thought before. Fast-forward a couple of years, and the next shock occurred on that magical night, the one that never seemed to end. The first shock made me question myself. The second introduced me to pain on a first-name basis. But in its own twisted way, it gave me some clarity. I couldn't claim that I fully understood myself yet, but I had unearthed something important. I had the ability to endure. I had the ability to push through pain and persevere, especially for things I cared about.

Qualifying for Boston was certainly something that I cared about. It had eluded me for almost a decade now, but I was ready to do my share of pushing and persevering to get to it.

A dream delayed is not a dream denied; it's just waiting for your better version.

In the days following the 100-kilometer night, I struggled to find the same motivation or joy that I usually associated with running. I wondered what was wrong with me. After having run 100 kilometers through that night, every "usual" run had started feeling trivial perhaps. At the end of each run, I would go back home with a strange, hollow feeling, comparing that day's run to the gigantic "once-in-a-lifetime run" I had done a few days ago.

At a philosophical level, it sometimes felt that the act of running was like a big pot of joy, which was designed to be used judiciously. The nectar was supposed to be extracted and savored bit by bit, day after day. I had made the classic mistake of extracting it all in one go, rendering it completely empty and incapable of offering any more joy. I sometimes wished I had never done that 100-kilometer run, for it had left me with a hollow feeling that running could not offer anything that I hadn't already experienced. But then, I reminded myself, there was still one thing that the act of running had to offer. I still had to qualify for the Boston Marathon, and that was motivation enough for me to lace up every evening, despite all the distracting thoughts I was struggling to make sense of.

In the hope of taking yet another stab at the coveted BQ, I signed up for the New Delhi Marathon. The event was scheduled for February 2022, so I had a good five months for preparation. In the past, I had made several attempts to crack the coveted BQ benchmark. The closest I had come was around five minutes shy of the qualification target. Sounds tantalizingly close, doesn't it? But in marathon math, it isn't.

Shaving off five minutes from one's best full-marathon timing calls for a disciplined approach. So, I vowed to start all over again. This time, I swore off all drama. No stunts. No last-minute experiments. I promised I would train like a monk—albeit a sweaty, slightly delusional monk with a GPS watch.

I made a conscious effort to snap out of the post-100-kilometer-run blues. I mentally elevated myself to a zone where I was content with just getting the basics right, blindly trusting the process. When you do something like that, the most important thing is the belief that while your actions may not show any visible improvement day after day, the process will slowly but surely nudge you along the right path. I was happily falling in love with the process again. I was no longer consumed by the dream of qualifying for Boston. The joy of doing the basics right every single day was becoming more important than the thought of BQ itself, and I was happy with that mindset shift.

Over the next five months, I religiously stuck to the plan. However, there was one run—just one—where I quit early. I had aimed to run 32 kilometers that day, but around the 26-kilometer mark, my mental demons took over and I decided to quit earlier than planned. It was quite unlike me, and I am not sure why I allowed myself to do that. I reflected upon it for several days. I couldn't find any reasons—maybe it was out of boredom; maybe I slipped into that gray zone where the force of attraction from the dark side triumphed. I was quite upset, and I vowed never to let it happen again. To eliminate any possibility of a repeat, I started to plan my long runs such that I would go half the planned distance in a direction away from home, and only then take a U-turn to get back home. *"That would leave me with no option but to keep running all the way to reach back home and complete the planned distance,"* I thought. The idea worked well, and I never aborted any run midway thereafter.

> *You can't always silence your inner quitter, but you can certainly outsmart it. Sometimes, the best way to stay the course is to remove all exits.*

By February, I felt ready. But then again, I had felt ready before. This time, though, I didn't just feel trained; I felt transformed. Older. Calmer. Less fiery, but more grounded. The runner in me had matured over the years.

Another BQ attempt—a "sincere" one this time

February 20, 2022, race day

Standing at the start line, I quietly observed the frenzy and excitement around me. It was all very familiar. Yet, there was something different in the way I felt that day.

As a novice runner, I used to put in every effort to be at the front of the pack of runners, thinking that staying ahead of the crowd would save me a few precious minutes. But here I was, happy and comfortable, standing at the far end of the pack with hundreds of runners ahead of me. I had no energy or desire to struggle with the crowd to get ahead of them.

Back in the day, just before the race kickoff, I would vigorously jump on the spot, dancing to the tunes of my adrenaline rush. That was not the case anymore. I was no longer the young amateur runner, ready to explode my way through the course. I was happy to flow and gradually find my way. As a young runner, I always had the urge to untie and tie my shoelaces one last time just before the race commenced. I didn't feel the need to do that either.

For an event with that kind of energy and frenzy, I was rather somber in that moment. The runner in me had mellowed over the years.

The countdown started: "Five, Four, Three, Two, One … Let's run, Delhi!"

As I crossed the start line, I murmured to myself, "Sincere BQ attempt today."

Amidst all the subtle shifts I was noticing, I noticed the change in the tone of my self-talk too. The Sundeep of yesteryears would have confidently murmured "Come on, Champ! BQ today," punching the air with his fist before making a splash through the start line. That was no longer the case. The confident (or maybe somewhat arrogant!) "BQ today" had made way for "Sincere BQ attempt today." I am not sure when and why that shift happened, but for some inexplicable reason, I was happy that it had happened. I wondered if my failed BQ attempts over the years had anything to do with it.

> *The journey humbles you, and sometimes in that humility, "sincere attempt" feels stronger than "must win."*

One of the aspects that I cherish the most about running a marathon is the downtime it offers. For a few hours, there is nothing to distract you—no phone calls, no Instagram reels, no deliverables, no household chores—just you and your thoughts. For the next couple of hours, I ran on the beautiful roads of Delhi, allowing my thoughts to sway across space and time. I thought about everything—the pranks I used pull on my grandmother, the petty fights with my sister, the way my parents always stood by me, the way I proposed to my wife, the classes I bunked in my college days, the moment I held my kid in my arms for the first time, the way Sachin used to destroy the opposition's bowling—I thought of almost every memory worth thinking about, and a few worth forgetting, which I had not been able to forget over the years.

I had almost forgotten about the "Sincere BQ attempt today" that I had started the run with. I kept running, merrily immersed in my thoughts, enjoying the state of trance I had slipped into.

Around the 37-kilometer mark, I noticed a man in the crowd holding a placard that read, "Five more to go!" That placard suddenly brought my attention back to the run. I glanced at my watch to check how I was doing. I had been on the road for about 2 hours and 47 minutes. I did some quick mental math to check how much time I had to possibly qualify for Boston: 22 minutes to knock off the remaining 5-odd kilometers. I was tantalizingly close to something that I had been chasing and missing for so long.

I thought about it for a minute, almost checking with myself if I had the ammunition to go for the kill. It was touch and go. I knew I would either make it or miss it by less than a minute. That brief moment jostled me out of the state of trance, almost hurtling me back a few years when a BQ was a matter of life and death.

"Game on!" I yelled like a deranged gladiator, probably startling a few bystanders.

As I crossed the 41-kilometer mark, I checked the watch again. I still had about five minutes to go. I was now sure to miss the distance narrowly. I had been in that position way too many times, just that this time I would miss a BQ.

"No, can't let it go from here," I murmured and pushed myself as hard as I could. I could feel my head spinning, and I was aware that I was pushing myself very close to the point of breakdown. A part of me warned me to slow down.

> **me**: *"It is not cool to faint on the track. Just slow down and let it go."*
>
> **ME**: *"Shut up, you moron! I am too close to let it go now."*

Before the internal banter got too messy, I muted both voices and just ran.

The finish line was in sight now, barely 100 meters away. I looked at the big digital watch at the finish line. It read 3:09:15.

I sprinted like a man possessed and crossed the finish line in 3:09:36, with 24 seconds to spare.

It was a gigantic moment for me, one that I had been chasing for almost a decade. Yet, now that it happened, I had no energy to react or celebrate. I was struggling to control tears. All I needed was solitude, a few moments with myself. I gingerly limped to a quiet corner in the stadium, one where no one could watch me. I collapsed on the grass, lay there with my legs and arms wide open, and looked at the beautiful, blue sky, not worrying about the happy tear that finally found its way out.

I was a Boston Qualifier. Finally.

It had taken me 2,646 days since I ran my first half marathon.

And in that quiet, tear-streaked moment under the sky, I finally understood what people mean when they say, *"All it takes is ALL you've got."*

Key Messages

i. Knowing others is wisdom; knowing yourself is liberation.

For years, I took pride in reading the world around me, analyzing others with a quiet confidence. But it took the solitude of a long run and the stillness after a storm to realize how little I knew myself. Pain became the unlikely mirror in which I caught a clearer glimpse of who I really was and what I was capable of enduring when it mattered.

ii. There is no shortcut in life.

The only way to get better at anything is practice. Resist the temptation of getting trapped in the vicious cycle of complaining about lack of time. If you are truly passionate about something, you will find a way to make time. At the end of the day (or should I say, at the beginning of the day), only you can get yourself out of bed at 5 a.m.

iii. A fire should burn, but it shouldn't blind.

Over time, the frenzied urgency to prove myself began to mellow. I no longer needed to stand at the front of the pack or punch the air before a race. I didn't feel the need to shout my goals aloud—a quiet murmur to myself was enough. With every failed attempt, every honest effort, something inside me softened. I was no longer running to conquer. I was running to understand. And that shift from being a fiery go-getter to becoming a grounded seeker changed not just the way I ran, but the way I lived.

iv. All it takes is ALL you've got.

It took me 2,646 days after I started running to qualify for Boston. Not because I didn't want it badly enough earlier, but because some milestones don't yield to urgency. They yield to patience, grind, and endurance. If you're willing to push through the ups and downs along the way, something eventually gives.

THE SPIRIT OF LONG-DISTANCE RUNNING TRIUMPHS

(2023–2025)

"There will come a time when you believe everything is finished; that will be the beginning."

—Louis L'Amour

14

NOT EVERY SETBACK IS THE END

The battered warrior gets back on his feet

January 15, 2023

YOU never know how strong you are until being strong is your only option. Trust me, there are easier ways to learn this truth than lying face down on a hotel room floor in Mumbai.

I had been on the floor for God knows how long. Time plays weird games with your head when you don't have a watch. I tried to guess the time based on external cues, wondering how people did it in ancient times—probably by looking at the sun, animal behavior, or sheer witchcraft. I noticed that the sun was out and it was well past the break of dawn. I also noticed that runners on the road were now moving in the opposite direction, which meant that they were on their way back. Quick math told me it had been over three hours since the start of the race.

Running for three hours straight is brutal. Lying motionless for three hours? Somehow worse.

I had accepted my fate by then. I wasn't going to run on the beautiful streets of Mumbai that morning. Fine. My mind suddenly shifted to the more immediate concern.

"I need to find a way to pick myself up. I have a flight to catch in a few hours," I thought.

Also, not to be dramatic, but I was also starving to death by then. We runners need food all the time. We are essentially large toddlers with hyperactive metabolisms. We burn fuel faster than a bonfire. I knew that if I didn't get up soon, I'd have the double whammy of excruciating pain and raging hunger—not a combination any doctor would recommend.

I tried to move. Tiny movements. Just the essentials. To my horror, the pain was still at full blast. For a second, I wondered if this was how I was going out, not in a blaze of glory on the marathon course, but face down next to a king-size bed, abandoned by fate and my lumbar spine.

"No, that won't happen. Someone will surely break open the door and find me on the floor before then," I reasoned. I felt a sudden relief. It is fascinating what a positive thought can do in moments of stress.

I knew something had to give. I continued trying different postures to get up. After a few failed attempts, my pain and I started to develop an agreement. We were no longer strangers, and despite our mutual dislike, we were beginning to find ways to get along, like two bitter coworkers who have to collaborate to survive the workday.

Summoning every shred of courage, I pried my palms off the ground, grabbed the window handle, and pulled myself into an upright position.

The battered warrior was up. I was ecstatic yet devastated.

What lies within us is often stronger than what stands against us. We just need to dig deep enough to discover it.

The human body is probably the most adaptable machinery God ever created. In normal circumstances, it is designed to operate in a particular way, but if the circumstances are abnormal, it finds a workaround. It's almost like the parts of the body operate like a team. If one part is out of order, another part rises to the occasion to do more than its fair share and keeps the machine working (until the machine permanently breaks down one day!).

Next, I had to figure out a way to take baby steps.

My first goal was to reach my mobile phone, then the hotel reception, then the airport, and then finally back home, in Gurugram.

I tried to make tiny movements to check what gait might be acceptable to my disturbed back. Any attempt to take a usual step forward triggered excruciating pain.

After a bit of experimentation, I figured out a working formula.

Left foot forward. Weird torso rotation in an elliptical path, with arms hanging outward. Drag rear foot forward. Repeat.

I may or may not be exaggerating that a bit. I can't be sure, for I never watched myself walk in that room. But even after discounting any unintended exaggeration, I probably looked like a malfunctioning robot from a low-budget sci-fi movie.

Anyway, the robot had a mission now: get home by repeating those movements. A shiver ran down my spine.

After getting up, I moved my neck through the full range of motion, as if to check for any changes in the room. Everything was the same, except my back and me. Yet, the room had a very different vibe compared to the previous day.

The first thing to catch my attention was a can of Volini spray lying next to the LCD screen. Gold. Runners never travel without it. I'd never needed that magical can of false hope as much as I needed it in that moment.

Then, I saw my phone, lying tantalizingly close to the side table. I needed that too. I needed to call Japneet. If all had gone well that morning, this would have been my time to call her to share my run timing.

I noticed the banana and energy gels lying on the other side of the bed. I was starving and desperately needed to get hold of that banana too.

I also noticed my colorful running gear elegantly placed on one of the beds, mocking me. That was one thing that I surely didn't need. I wondered if I would ever need it again. It's tough to know when you're walking like a malfunctioning robot.

Every item in the room—the phone, banana, Volini spray, and pride—came at a heavy premium. I had to decide which item to get to first.

For a moment, it felt like one of those childhood logic puzzles:

"A man in pain is trapped in a room with a Volini spray, banana, and mobile phone, but he cannot move. How does he escape?"

I ditched the puzzle, robot-shuffled to the phone, and called Japneet.

"Hello, how did it go?" her voice exuded excitement and anticipation.

"I didn't go."

Awkward silence.

"What do you mean?"

No reply.

"What happened? Please say something."

"I got up with a sharp pain in the back this morning and have largely been immobile since then."

"How bad is it?"

"I didn't go to the event, so you can imagine," I replied with a nervous chuckle.

A few more moments of awkward silence.

"You stay right there. I will take the first flight and come over."

"Not a good idea. Even in the best-case scenario, it would take you several hours. I can't imagine staying in this state in this room for so long. I desperately need to get out of here."

"Can you go see a doctor?"

"I have been on the floor for four hours. It took me that long to get to my mobile. It's unlikely I can go to a doctor."

"What do you mean you have been on the floor? Please tell me exactly what happened."

"I will explain everything when I get back."

"Let me make a few calls and get some help to your room."

"That won't work either. This hotel is right on the race route. All traffic routes are closed till 2 p.m."

"How will you board the flight in this state?"

Another awkward pause.

"I will see you in the evening," I replied and hung up.

I realized I still had to kill a few hours before the race routes opened up for general traffic. I looked around the room with a complete absence of purpose.

Eventually, I zeroed in on my next critical mission: the banana.

Baby steps. Literally. I slid down slowly like a piece of toast in a vertical toaster, grabbed the banana, and gobbled it down in one savage gulp.

Now came the moral dilemma: What should I do with the peel?

There was no way I was going to take painful steps to get to the dustbin. I thought for a moment and decided to take a shot at the dustbin. I missed the shot, and the banana peel landed on the floor. On any other day, I would have fixed it, but in that moment, I couldn't care less.

The peel lay crumpled on the floor, the ultimate metaphor for my condition.

Next, I called up reception to get some help. The same chirpy lady answered the phone.

"Hello, Sir, good afternoon!"

"Good afternoon."

"How was your run, Sir?"

I thought for a moment about how to respond to her.

"Could I get a few painkillers?"

Awkward silence for a few seconds.

"Sure, Sir, I will have them sent right away."

"Thank you."

A few minutes later, an older gentleman—my literal savior—showed up with medicine. Seeing my state, he offered to help me pack. I almost hugged him. He neatly folded my running gear, zipped my bags, and arranged for a cab. He even helped me hobble to the car.

As I walked past the hotel lobby, the lady at the reception looked at me with a mixture of guilt, pity, and horror. She didn't have the courage to ask me what had happened, and I didn't have the energy to explain either. I can't stand the sight of someone looking at me with sympathy. So, I waved to her and quickly looked away.

With assistance from the cab driver and the housekeeping angel, the battered warrior made it into the cab.

I was on my way to the airport.

Mission "Escape Mumbai" was officially underway.

Upright (sort of), breathing (definitely), home (finally)

The TMM is probably India's biggest running event. In the build-up to race day, the entire city transforms into a runners' playground. Enthusiastic amateurs and slick professionals alike pound the pavements of Mumbai. The iconic Marine Drive turns into a parade of dreams in motion. Cafés buzz with running plans instead of gossip. At airports and railway stations, runners are everywhere, duffle bags slung over their shoulders and compression socks peeking out from under their jeans. Even taxi drivers, without missing a beat, politely ask, "Here for TMM?" as they lift your bags into the trunk.

The whole city hums with athletic energy that's downright infectious. I had fallen in love with that vibe back in 2015, during my first full marathon in Mumbai—the day I officially became a marathoner.

As the cab inched toward the airport, I blankly stared out of the window, soaking in that electric vibe—the gentle sea breeze, the kilometer markers along the road, the giant TMM hoardings, runners proudly flashing their finisher medals. It all felt so familiar, yet painfully out of reach this time.

I remembered my first appearance at the event. I was an amateur back then. I still am, but a relatively experienced one. Back then, I had joyfully jogged along the streets of Mumbai playing the Bollywood classic, *"...ye hai Mumbai meri jaan..."* in my mind. I was starting an exciting journey back then. That beautiful journey was coming to an end eight years later, ironically at the same place where it started. I closed my eyes, somberly feeling the gentle breeze on my face.

Before I knew it, the cab pulled up at the airport.

As I "robot-walked" into the terminal, I became acutely aware of my condition. Very few things in life can draw both sympathy and laughter at the same time. My gait certainly qualified as one on those things—left foot forward, slow elliptical torso rotation, arms flailing awkwardly like broken windshield wipers, rear foot forward; I knew the drill well by now.

I kept my head down and shuffled along.

"Are you okay, Sir?" asked an Indigo flight attendant.

"Well, as you can see, No!" I replied as politely as I could.

"Do you need some help?"

I smiled. "I would be grateful if you could help me board the flight."

"Sure, Sir," he replied as he took the suitcase from me.

The poor gentleman slowed down to match my tortoise-like speed. He walked me through check-in and security, using his magical airline privileges to let me skip queues. It was a huge help. I'm not sure I would have ever had the ego-free courage to ask for help on my own. Sometimes, life just sends you the right people at the right moments.

A little while later, I shuffled into the aircraft. One painful step closer to home.

The only thing worrying me now was the flight itself. Sitting was, by far, the worst possible posture for my wrecked back. In the cab, I had at least managed to recline sideways like a wounded soldier. Here, I wasn't sure how I'd survive.

I politely asked the air hostess if I could stand during the flight. She disappeared for a few moments to check, then returned.

"During take-off and landing, you must be seated, Sir. But after that, you're welcome to stand at the rear near the galley," she said apologetically.

"Don't be sorry. That's all I need," I smiled.

I have always been an anxious flier. Even mild turbulence is enough to make "flying anxiety" visible on my face. I usually try to close my eyes as a way of coping with it. That evening though, my mind was preoccupied: how I would manage pain during the journey, how I would get out of the aircraft after landing, how I would make my way to the cab, would someone help me with my luggage—there were just too many thoughts. Unsurprisingly, not once did I think about turbulence that evening.

Pain has a way of reorganizing your fear hierarchy.

I leaned against a wall at the back of the aircraft and stared out of a tiny window for almost the entire flight, lost in thought. I was dead tired by then. I needed a few hours of solitude, just being with myself, in the safe environment of my study. But that was still a few hours away.

It was well past 11 p.m. by the time I limped home. It had been a brutally hard day, but somehow, I had managed to keep moving. For that, I gave myself a tiny, invisible medal.

Going through unexpected physical pain can be tough, but watching your loved ones watch you go through that pain can be tougher. For some reason, it makes me feel completely vulnerable. So, I always try to hide any challenge that I may be going through from my family. Their getting to know about it only adds to my woes.

I rang the doorbell.

Japneet opened the door. She stared at me, half worried, half relieved. I shuffled inside without a word. She didn't say anything either.

We just ... stared at each other.

I could feel all the questions swirling inside her. I was scrambling inside my head, trying to figure out the least traumatic version of the story to tell her.

The silence stretched until finally she asked, in her signature way, "Did you eat anything?"

The question almost made me laugh. I had survived the entire day on a banana. And yet here I was, upright (sort of), breathing (definitely), and home (finally). No wonder bananas are a runner's best friend.

"Well, no. Nothing since I had a banana in the morning,"

She disappeared into the kitchen and returned with a steaming plate of *rajma-chawal,* my absolute favorite. I devoured it like there was no tomorrow.

"How is the pain now?"

"Not very different from this morning," I admitted. "When it first hit, it completely blindsided me. I was stranded for hours."

I could see her face tense up.

"But during the day, I figured out a few hacks," I added quickly, trying to lighten the mood.

We were both thinking about the same thing.

Neither of us wanted to say it out loud.

Finally, she broke the silence.

"The Boston Marathon is still three months away. I'm sure you'll be fine by then."

I wanted to believe it. I *wanted* to.

But I had lived the day. I knew how deep the damage ran.

"I'm not sure," I said quietly.

We just exchanged a helpless smile.

No more words were needed.

The day ended the way it had begun—not with a bang, but with a whimper. I had always imagined this day would be special—my final big race before Boston. Instead, it turned out to be the day I realized I might not even make it to Boston.

> *Life is what unfolds in the moments between your plans, making the journey far more unpredictable than the destination.*

The BQ I had fought so hard for? It was slipping away before I could even celebrate it properly.

I hadn't spelled it out to Japneet, but deep down, I knew. I'd have to start over, qualify all over again. That is, *if* I could ever run again.

As I closed my eyes that night, a line I had read somewhere floated back into my mind:

"Life is what happens to you while you're busy making other plans."

Turns out that it's absolutely true.

Key Messages

i. **Life doesn't take permissions. It just moves.**
That fateful day in Mumbai wasn't part of the plan. I had trained, prepared, and visualized a very different outing in my final race before the coveted Boston run. But life, in its own quiet way, reminded me that it doesn't run by my calendar or ambition. It moves forward—indifferent, invincible—and the only choice I have is whether I move with it or stay stranded in protest.

ii. **What we think are our limits are often just the starting points of who we really are.**
We are all infinitely more resilient than what we are consciously aware of. Unlocking this potential is a bit of science, a bit of art, and a lot of dogged perseverance. It is contingent upon our ability to look within and the willingness to venture into the zone of discomfort. That day, I didn't conquer a race or smash a personal best. I just survived, one banana, one shuffle, one awkward smile at a time. And somehow, that took more strength than any finish line ever had.

15

HOPE, MY FRIEND, IS A GOOD THING

Time to hang in there

I HAVE always been averse to the idea of seeing a doctor or taking medicine. I probably got that mindset from my father. No matter how badly he's hurting, the moment someone suggests a check-up, he changes the subject, as if it is impolite to even mention his health concerns. Over the years, I've picked up the same habit. For me, seeing a doctor was always a last resort, and I took a weird sort of pride in that mindset.

But pride is like a rubber band—stretch it long enough and it will eventually snap.

The next morning, I asked Japneet to take me to the doctor.

Looking at my robotic walk, the doctor asked me to get an MRI done—my first ever. As I lay in the MRI machine, it felt like my entire world came crashing in. From running joyfully under the open sky to being mechanically slid into the MRI chamber, a lot seemed to have changed within a day. Not an upgrade for sure.

Then the machine started making a hostile noise. Tik, Tik, Tok, Tik, Tik, Tok ...

I wasn't ready for that noise. Or the claustrophobia. Or the panic. I started spiraling. Then, as I do during turbulence on flights, I shut my eyes and pretended none of it was happening.

I shut it all out.

When the doctor finally looked at my scan, my heart was thudding like it wanted to file an official complaint. I wanted him to say, "It's all good, just rest and you will be fine."

Instead, he squinted at the screen and said, "You should forget about running again."

"Sorry, what?"

"I mean you've pushed your body beyond its limits. This," he pointed at the scan, "is the result. You've screwed yourself royally."

"Is this how you talk to all your patients?" I asked.

He looked mildly surprised by my tone.

"We're done here," I said, standing up. "Thank you."

"Listen, there's no need to ...."

Japneet cut in. "Didn't you hear him? We're done."

And out we walked.

Yes, we had attitude. But he had a pathetic bedside manner. Maybe he was right—100 half marathons in 100 days, a spontaneous 100-kilometer night run *were* a bit much. But a touch of grace wouldn't have killed him.

I left the clinic with two things: a damaged back and a reinforced dislike for doctors.

I don't intend to brag about it, but I think we long-distance runners have a weird superpower: We're fantastic at ignoring pain. When every cell is begging you to stop, you learn how to trick your brain into taking just one more step. Toward the end of a marathon, when your body is staging a full-on mutiny, your inner voice gently lies to you: *Just one more step, my friend.*

Your poor brain, bless it, believes that inner voice.

And once we take that all-important next step, it suddenly fades away into the past, and the step ahead takes centerstage. We once again convince our mind to do it one more time, and then one more time, all the way until we reach our destination. Every step is a struggle. There is a constant tussle: Our physical sensations try to hold us back, and that inner voice keeps asking for one more step.

That's exactly what I did after the MRI. "Just get through today," I told myself.

Then the next day. Then the next.

Every night, I slept with the hope that when I woke up in the morning, the pain would have miraculously disappeared. Every morning, I awoke with the same pain. Days turned into weeks, and weeks into months. The pain stuck around like an uninvited guest who doesn't get the hint.

> *Progress doesn't always roar. Sometimes it limps, breathes heavily, and whispers, "Not yet."*

In response, my body developed a new mobility framework for daily chores. Bending was out of question. Fortunately for me, I had a decade of lunges under my belt. Need to pick something up? Drop into a lunge like a fitness influencer doing a product demo. Sitting? Again, a no-go. My work involves a lot of sitting, so I adapted. I took frequent walking breaks, or lay face down in cobra pose, typing like a human pretzel. It wasn't graceful, but it worked.

A part of me made peace with this strange new reality. The

other part kept grieving. Running had quietly exited my life, and I hadn't even had the chance to say goodbye.

And now, the Boston Marathon was just a week away.

My cherished Boston memory—lonely, but mine!

April 17, 2023, the day of the 127th Boston Marathon

This was supposed to be *the day*. I'd imagined it for years: high-fives at the finish line, medal selfies, and a joyful celebration with family and friends. Instead, what panned out in reality was very different. I was sitting thousands of miles away, staring blankly at my digital race pass.

The thing I had trained and bled for was just a digital memory. I kept staring at my digital entry pass for the 127th Boston Marathon.

SUNDEEP
SINGH

Bib Number: 10108

Date of Birth: 29-January-83

Gender: Male

Bus Load Time: 7:30 AM

Wave: White

Corral: 3

Start Time: 10:25 AM

Please present this pass along with a GOVERNMENT ISSUED PHOTO ID at the Boston Marathon Expo to receive your bib number.

The prized possession (the Boston Marathon admit card) I earned after years of hard work

Despite what panned out, it was a very special day for me. It was my Boston Marathon. I had earned it after years of hard work. That mattered. So, I decided to celebrate, in my own weird way, by visiting the Tau Devi Lal Stadium in Gurugram, the place where it had all started. I went at noon when I knew it would be empty. I didn't want company. I wanted closure.

Not all triumphs need a podium. Some are best honored in quiet reflection.

It was my first visit in nearly four months. I walked the track slowly, soaking in the heat, the silence, the nostalgia. The vibe felt different, maybe because I wasn't running anymore, or maybe because I wasn't the same person anymore.

I was limping. But I was walking. And that, at least, was something.

As I strolled around, a lot of thoughts crossed my mind.

I'd been running for almost ten years. I always knew there would be an expiration date. That's just the deal. Over the years, age and physical exertion had taken a toll. It is natural, and sooner or later, age catches up with everyone. There has never been an exception; there never will be one. Why, then, did I feel bad about it? It was the ultimate truth of life that was beginning to unfold. I tried to convince myself that acceptance was the only way forward. The only choice I had was to do that either gracefully or resentfully. They say make hay while the sun shines. I had certainly made hay during my sunshine years.

Still, it hurt.

Every morning, my sensible voice said, *"Accept it. Move on."*

Every morning, the stubborn "ME," the one that signs up for 100-kilometer runs just to see what happens, kept pushing back.

"This is not how all of this was supposed to end," it argued.

All giant egos are reluctant to let go of their cherished possessions. They say that even the magnificent Titanic stood motionless for a few moments before it finally went down.

Was I experiencing *my* Titanic moment?

I didn't know. My brain was too foggy to tell.

But as I continued to walk around, my thoughts were suddenly diverted.

What do people really mean when they say, "He was destined to be in this situation?"

It sounds poetic, but it is also kind of passive, as if you're just a character in someone else's story. It implies a lack of control, as if cosmic powers beyond your control are conspiring to get you into a situation. It feels like destiny is a matter of chance, and you cannot do anything about it. It nudges you toward the ultimate path of acceptance: This is your fate. Accept it. Accept who you are, where you are, how you are, because you cannot do anything about it anyway.

And for a while, I did accept it. I let go of resistance. I surrendered to circumstance.

But the idea kept gnawing at me. Was destiny really a matter of chance, or could it be shaped, step by step, thought by thought? That's when I remembered an old Chinese quote I had come across long ago. It had sounded wise back then, almost like an instruction manual to reclaim the right to your destiny:

"Watch your thoughts, they become your words; watch your words, they become your actions; watch your actions, they become your habits; watch your habits, they become your character; watch your character, it becomes your destiny."

If this chain of transformation from thoughts to destiny is true, then destiny cannot just be a matter of chance. One should be able to influence destiny, at least to some extent, by controlling one's thoughts.

I wondered which of these schools of thought was true. Or maybe like all things in life, it was not one or the other. Was it, again, an instance of "It depends?"

I do think it depends; it depends on the lens you are looking through. If you consider the ultimate truth of life, then you have to accept that you will die one day. No matter what thoughts you cultivate, you cannot change that truth. But if you think about the path you take to that ultimate truth, you can certainly influence it by altering your thoughts.

You may not control every outcome, but you hold the pen to your story through your mindset and choices.

"I don't like the path I am currently on. I need to change this path by changing my thoughts," I concluded as I casually slowed down to occupy a comfortable spot.

They say running mirrors life. I was beginning to see the reflection more clearly.

As I continued to reflect, my attention went back to an old wall painting in our kitchen when I was a kid. It displayed a beautiful poem printed next to a pair of footprints on a beach. I'd seen it a hundred times, but never really read it. I couldn't explain from where that inconsequential wall painting came back to my conscious mind, but I was thinking about it, nonetheless.

"One night I dreamed a dream.
As I was walking along the beach with my Guide.
Across the dark sky flashed scenes from my life.
For each scene, I noticed two sets of footprints in the sand,
One belonging to me and one to my Guide.

After the last scene of my life flashed before me,
I looked back at the footprints in the sand.
I noticed that many times along the path of my life,
especially at the very lowest and saddest times,
there was only one set of footprints.

This really troubled me, so I asked my Guide about it.
"Guide, you said once I decided to follow you,
You'd walk with me all the way.
But I noticed that during the saddest and most troublesome times of my life,
there was only one set of footprints.
I don't understand why, when I needed You the most, You would leave me."

He whispered, "My precious child, I love you and will never leave you.
Never, ever, during your trials and testings.
When you saw only one set of footprints,
It was then that I carried you."

I'd always thought of it as cheesy fridge poetry. But sitting alone on that stadium track, I realized it wasn't cheesy at all. I looked around at the empty lanes, the warm concrete, the big quiet.

Could it be true? I wondered. I hoped I was being carried by someone through those days.

A glimmer of hope

The easiest way to start a conversation with a runner is to ask them about their running. Often, this innocent query unleashes a deluge of detail—splits, pace zones, tempo sessions, lactate thresholds, VO2 max values, and a few acronyms thrown in for extra flair. It's a bit like someone asking on a Monday morning, "How was your weekend?" Nobody's actually asking for a scene-by-scene replay, but some people don't get it. They treat the question as an invitation to submit a memoir.

We runners are guilty of the same. "How's your running coming along?" might be a polite filler during a conversation, but for us, it's a wide-open door to a TED talk.

That evening, however, things were different. We were out for dinner with close family friends.

"So, how's your running coming along?" Reena asked casually as we waited around a table for the chef to do his magic.

"It has come to a complete halt," I replied.

Everyone paused, caught off guard by my bluntness. Everyone except Japneet.

"What do you mean?" Reena asked, leaning forward, confusion on her face.

"I mean exactly what I said," I shrugged and gave them the rundown of the TMM debacle and the doctor's bleak verdict.

"What exactly did the doctor say?"

"He said I am screwed and I should forget about running again."

Silence. The kind that hangs uncomfortably in the air.

"I know a very good sports injury specialist," Reena offered, her tone earnest. "Dr. Mueller. He is of German origin. He runs the AktivHealth rehab centers. You should see him."

"No, thanks. I'm done with doctors. They're good for nothing," I snapped, a little too sharply.

Another awkward silence. Clearly, I was winning at the dinner conversation.

"He's very hurt," Japneet interjected gently, holding my hand. "But Reena, please send me the details. I'll convince him to go."

A few days later, we were at Dr. Mueller's rehabilitation center in Vasant Vihar. I walked in with my hopes buried under a thick coat of cynicism. I wasn't even sure whom I was trying to fool.

As we waited, one of Dr. Mueller's colleagues conducted a thorough interrogation: nature of pain, timing, triggers, posture, almost everything other than my blood group. He could have written a doctoral thesis based on that consultation. I answered as candidly as possible.

"I'll brief Dr. Mueller now. He'll be with you shortly," he said, leaving me alone with my unease.

Moments later, a cheerful, athletic man entered the room. I recognized Dr. Mueller instantly from my numerous Google searches.

He gave me a friendly pat on the back. "So, did you run this morning, my friend?"

"I wouldn't be here if I had been in a position to do that."

He smiled knowingly, "Fair point."

"I'm going to examine you now, if you're okay taking off your T-shirt and doing a few movements?"

"Sure, Sir."

"Before we begin, may I say, impressive physique. You've clearly been diligent with your training."

Never let the disappointments of the past close the door to new possibilities.

"But what good is a runner's body if it doesn't run anymore?"

"What good is my profession if I can't get you running again?" he said very softly while scribbling on his notepad, as if not intending for me to hear it. I heard it, though. And just like that, he became my best friend.

The beaming smile on his face gradually made way for a

focused look as he got ready to practice his craft. He asked me to make a few specific movements.

"Left leg up, please, right leg up, please, walk forward, lie on the bed and raise your leg, turn sideways, raise your left leg sideways please, now the other side ..."

He went on for a few minutes. I followed every instruction like a devoted disciple. Best friends don't let best friends down.

Once done, he scribbled some notes and looked up.

"When is your next running event?"

I couldn't believe what he'd said.

I blinked. "Excuse me?"

"Your next event?"

"Well, I have not been tracking the event dates of late, but there is a major annual event coming up in Delhi around mid-October. That's about seven weeks away."

"Perfect," he said. "Let's aim for you to start slow runs in three weeks. For October, register for the 10-kilometer race. Take it easy. We'll gradually build back to marathons. My colleague will guide you with daily exercises, and I'd like you to visit us once or twice a week. Sounds good?"

"You have given me a lifeline, Sir. Anything that gets me back on track is doable."

That brief meeting changed everything. He had given me the one thing I hadn't dared to feel: hope.

"Remember, Red, hope is a good thing, maybe the best of things. And no good thing ever dies."

That line from *The Shawshank Redemption* echoed in my head as I walked out.

A new lease of life

The recovery sessions at the rehab center started paying off almost immediately. Within a week, the pain had reduced significantly. The stiff, robotic quality of my gait began to loosen. I wasn't exactly gliding like Eliud Kipchoge, the long-distance runner, but I no longer looked like a wound-up toy in distress.

And maybe, just maybe, the shift wasn't only physical. For the first time in months, my mind allowed itself to flirt with the possibility of progress. After what felt like forever, I believed something good could happen.

Hope, I've come to realize, is not just a feeling. It's a drug—a powerful, legal, life-saving drug. There's that old phrase, "Where there is life, there is hope." But I think the converse is equally true. Where there is hope, there is life. I was starting to feel alive again, thanks to Dr. Mueller and his quiet brand of optimism.

They say, "Where there is life, there is hope," but the converse is equally true!

As Dr. Mueller had planned, within three weeks, I was ready to lace up again—slow runs, nothing fancy.

It was a Friday evening.

I was warming up for a slow jog around the society loop—light drills, gentle stretches, trying to ease my body into motion without scaring it. As I worked through my routine, I noticed a lady walking toward me. Something told me that she would stop for a chat. I'd spent enough time on that loop to develop early-warning radar for social interactions. I looked away and continued with my warm-up drills.

Sure enough, as she passed by, she slowed down.

"Hi, my name is Gurleen."

"Hi, I am Sundeep."

"My husband and I often see you jogging here in the evenings."

"Yeah, I picked this hobby a few years ago and somehow managed to stick with it. Almost daily."

"My husband used to be a sprinter in college. His name is Sudeep. We've often thought of saying hello, but we didn't want to interrupt your run. It's the first time I've seen you not moving, so I thought I'd grab the moment."

"That's very thoughtful of you. But next time, don't hesitate to stop me."

She smiled. "Noted. Sudeep should be back from work any minute now. He usually joins me for these walks. If you're still around, we'll stop you."

"Please do. I'd love to meet a fellow runner."

Two laps later, I spotted Sudeep with her. I slowed down and walked over.

"Hi, Sudeep. It's good to know that you are a runner too."

"Yes, I used to be. Every time I see you running, I feel like joining in."

I was pleasantly surprised to notice the couple's warmth and friendliness. It was an easy, warm interaction, which, to be honest, is rare for me. I'm not the kind to open up to strangers mid-jog. But this felt different. Within minutes, we were trading notes about families, work, hobbies, and how both our names sounded like variations of each other.

I was mindful not to cool down too much during the chat. Muscles in recovery have the emotional stability of a teenager: You have to treat them gently or they throw tantrums.

"It's been great talking to you both," I said, easing back into motion. "Thanks for stopping me. I'm sure we'll bump into each other again very often."

"Absolutely," Sudeep replied. "And we'd love to join you on your runs, if that's alright."

"More than alright. Looking forward to it," I waved goodbye and resumed my run.

They both came across as simple, fun-loving people. To

be completely honest, I hate stopping for chit-chats during my running time. But connecting with Gurleen and Sudeep was different.

Soon, they joined me regularly for runs, bringing a kind of quiet joy to those loops. Weekend coffees followed, and then weekday badminton. On most days, I used to end up losing, partly because my movements were constrained and largely because he was a better player. I didn't mind losing those games as they were helping to restore my mobility. Each rally, each coffee, each laugh was stitching together a version of me that I'd lost sight of.

Here's the thing: You never undertake a solo journey in life. People appear, not always with grand entrances or spiritual music, but with small gestures, at the right time. Knowingly or unknowingly, your journey gets intertwined with that of people around you. This intertwining of paths impacts you in ways that may not be immediately apparent. Yet, every interaction, every incident is nudging you along a path. It feels like part of a script maintained by the higher power. Since you don't have access to that script, it is impossible to decipher it in real time. But sometimes, things begin to make sense in hindsight. I deliberately use the word "sometimes" to reflect my limitations in interpreting things. Over the years, I have realized that only when things suit me, they start making sense. Anything that doesn't suit me doesn't make sense even in hindsight, as if the only purpose for the world's existence is to gratify me. I easily forget that I am a small, inconsequential piece in the universe's unfathomably enormous jigsaw puzzle. Things happen, not with an intent to suit me or trouble me; they just happen. And the intellectual in me keeps trying to find patterns to explain "why" they happen.

The universe doesn't conspire for or against you; it simply flows. It takes a lifetime to understand that we are not the center of the script but just a tiny speck in the grander unfolding.

Yet, when things do suit me, I don't think about their significance. I merrily embrace the developments and feel blessed. That's exactly how I was feeling. A suggestion from Reena. Quiet confidence from Dr. Mueller. A simple hello from Gurleen. A game of badminton with Sudeep. All of it, somehow, felt orchestrated, like I was a line of code in some divine script and these moments were the patches and updates pulling me out of a bug. It felt like a part of God's mysterious script, a script that was gently nudging me back into motion.

"A body remains at rest, or in uniform motion, unless acted upon by an external force."

This is Newton's first law of motion, the Law of Inertia, for physical bodies. The beauty of these physics laws lies in their universal applicability—no exceptions, no preconditions, and certainly never a case of "it depends." Over time, I have come to believe that these laws may actually extend far beyond the physical world, to the emotional world if you will. It's hard to move until something, or someone, nudges you.

What if one day we find out that God had designed these laws to have a far broader relevance, almost like a fundamental paradigm underlying every perceivable stimulus, but as humans, we were limited in our abilities to interpret these laws? Consider Newton's third law of motion, for instance: *"Every action has an equal and opposite reaction."* Sounds suspiciously close to *"You reap what you sow,"* doesn't it? Maybe physics and philosophy are distant cousins speaking in different accents.

It's possible that the laws of motion weren't meant just for apples and planets, but for people, pain, and progress too.

But that's a topic for a different day.

In that phase of my life, I clearly saw the applicability of the Law of Inertia. For long, I had been in a state of rest. But the interactions with friends and family were providing me with the nudge I needed to get back into motion.

I was ready to start running again.

Key Messages

i. **Hope is not a feeling—it's a force.**
For the longest time, I had replaced hope with logic. If the body wasn't responding, what was the point of optimism? But then came a doctor who believed for me when I couldn't. Hope didn't shout. It whispered. And that whisper was enough to set things in motion again. I've realized that hope isn't a soft cushion we rest on—it is the spark that pushes us off the couch.

ii. **The right people arrive without ceremony, but with quiet purpose.**
You never undertake a solo journey in life. I realized this simple truth at the lowest point of my running journey. A conversation with a stranger on a running loop. A game of badminton. A suggestion at the right time. Life's best interventions don't come with grand music or dramatic lights. They come in the form of people who walk into your orbit, casually but meaningfully. Looking back, it's easy to believe they were always meant to be there—not to fix me, but to remind me that I wasn't alone on the journey.

16

IT ALL LIES WITHIN YOU

The gift of feeling alive, all over again

IT had been over a year since I last ran in a competitive race. The last time I'd signed up for one, it had turned into a nightmare on the streets of Mumbai.

After clawing my way back from injury, I wasn't quite sure how to approach my running. Sure, I had begun lacing up again, but I wasn't confident that my body was ready to go through the same grind it once endured. I found myself hesitating, wondering whether the effort to qualify for Boston all over again was even worth it. A part of me felt obligated to try because running in the Boston Marathon had been a long-standing dream. But dreams evolve. And I wasn't sure if this one still held the same shape.

Over the years, I've come to believe that the answers to our most pressing questions don't lie in books, conversations, or internet rabbit holes—they lie buried deep within us. We always *know*, don't we? Deep down, we carry quiet, unglamorous wisdom about what is right for us. But we spend a lifetime looking elsewhere. We ask friends and family. We search for validation, chase convenient logic, beg for signs, hunt for something we can point to—something rational enough to justify action. Meanwhile, the little inner voice doesn't stand a chance. It's too soft, too easily drowned by noise, doubt, and the illusion of clarity.

> *The answers we spend a lifetime seeking out there have been lying deep inside us all along.*

I don't claim to have turned into a Zen master, but somewhere along the way, I had changed. I had grown. And perhaps for the first time, I was ready to look inward with more honesty than ever before.

So, I asked myself: *"Is the Boston qualification what you truly want to run for?"*

No immediate *"yes."* No immediate *"no"* either. Just silence.

I probed further: *"Why do you run?"*

Again, no answer. Just deadly silence.

This time, I couldn't get away with my usual response. I couldn't tell myself, *"it's my me time,"* my go-to response when others ask the same question. That line works well in interviews and polite conversations. You can't lie to yourself with buzzwords. Not for long.

I was confused.

And yet, despite the brain fog, I kept showing up. Morning after morning, I stepped on the track, training for the next event I had signed up for, the Vedanta Delhi Half Marathon 2024.

October 20, 2024, Vedanta Delhi Half Marathon

As I made my way to the start line, I felt something swelling up inside me. Something emotional. Minutes before the gun went off, an old, familiar voice crept in with a question: *"Age is just a number,"* they say. *"Really?"* part of me scoffed. *"No, it is not just a number. I've been running for over a decade now, and I can feel the difference. I tire more easily. I get injured more often. I spend more time recovering than I do running. If that's not age, what is?"*

The run began.

Halfway through the run, I was still thinking about the same question. But something had shifted. The perspective had softened.

"Yes, I tire more easily, and sure, injuries visit more often than they used to. But I also know myself better now. I understand what matters. I've learned how to pace, not just my strides, but my life. I can push through pain longer. I can persevere harder. And more than anything, I can accept things with a grace that I never had in my 20s."

As I ran, clarity ran with me.

Age, I realized, is not just a number. But that's not a limitation; it's a blessing. It is the measure of how much life I've been gifted so far. Each year is a layer, each mile a memory. If our life is lived well, age makes us greater, not weaker. We often tie our self-worth to the wrong metrics—salary brackets, social status, square footage. But the real essence of life lays elsewhere—in moments, not milestones.

What truly matters in life can't be measured in metrics. It is felt deeply in simple moments.

It took me over 10 years of running—around stadiums, through city streets, and sometimes deep inside myself—to realize that truth. I didn't learn it at IIT or IIM. I learned it limping around the lanes of Gurugram, listening to my breath, watching the sun rise behind buildings.

The run eventually ended.

Strangely, I hadn't looked at my watch even once. And it wasn't a conscious decision. I just didn't care because time didn't seem important anymore. For the first time in a long time, the outcome didn't matter. Just the fact that I was running again felt enough.

Strangely enough, it turned out to be the fastest I had run at an event. I finished the run in 1 hour, 25 minutes, and 40 seconds.

Through the years, running has handed me every emotion on the spectrum. On some days, it makes me feel like an invincible warrior. On other days, it makes me want to lie on the floor and cry. It has given me ecstasy and deflation, clarity and confusion. It has made me feel deeply connected to the world, and then suddenly disconnected from everything and everyone. These emotions vary wildly in tone and texture, but they are all stitched together by one unmistakable thread: They make me feel alive.

So, as I crossed that finish line, I quietly closed my eyes. I thanked the higher power, whoever or whatever it may be, for giving me the luxury of feeling alive again. For allowing me to return to that precious state of being fully present, fully alive, and wholly free.

Maybe, just maybe, the answer I'd been searching for had started to emerge.

The joy of feeling alive and liberated

February 23, 2025, Apollo Tyres New Delhi Marathon (ATNDM)

Every full marathon I've run till date holds a special place in my heart. Each time I cross the finish line, I somehow feel "greater" than where I began, not in time or rank, but in spirit. Yet, on the eve of the ATNDM 2025, I found myself in a strange space. A quiet, unfamiliar resistance took hold of me. I didn't want to show up. No specific reason. Just an unsettling sense of reluctance. The viral fever I had developed during the week didn't help either.

Maybe I wasn't mentally ready. Maybe I was afraid. The idea of running another BQ race didn't stir me like it once did. It felt weighty, not in ambition, but in expectation. I seriously considered skipping the event. But an inner whisper kept echoing the personal code of conduct I have followed all my life: *"Not showing up is not an option. You break the rule once, and the cracks spread quietly, irreversibly. You become more susceptible to breaking that rule again."*

Not showing up is not an option. You break the rule once, and the cracks spread quietly, irreversibly. You become more susceptible to breaking that rule again.

The next morning, I stood at the start line at 4:00 a.m. sharp.

I vividly remembered the last time I ran the same race two years ago. It had been a glorious morning. I had qualified for Boston. It was special. I had been in peak form then, in both body and mind. But that was a different chapter. A lot had changed since then.

On this morning, I wasn't sure if I had the fire to chase that dream again or even the physical strength to try. As always, there was a council meeting going on in my head between familiar voices, stubbornly opinionated.

me: *"You are standing at the start line of a full marathon. This is reason enough to feel blessed."*

ME: *"Of course, I feel blessed."*

me: *"Good. Then I trust you won't try anything reckless today."*

ME: *"What do you mean?"*

me: *"I mean, don't forget you're still recovering. You had to ask your friend to tie your shoelaces this morning because you couldn't bend to tie them yourself. And you are down with fever too."*

ME: *"I know that. You don't need to remind me."*

me: *"Then promise me you're not thinking about a BQ today."*

Silence.

me: *"Your silence worries me. Say something."*

Still nothing.

me: *"If you were fully fit, this would be different. But today? You're nowhere close. Don't be stupid."*

ME (finally): *"I hate it when people defend their position using ifs and buts. I would rather gracefully accept an unfavorable outcome than try to hide in the garb of ifs and buts."*

me: *"What does that even mean?"*

ME (quietly, but firmly): *"Winning and losing might be context-sensitive. But trying? Trying doesn't need context. I'm okay with not qualifying today. But I'm not okay with not trying."*

me (exasperated): *"Why this obsession with BQ? Why can't you just move on?"*

ME: *"It's not about BQ anymore."*

Before the debate could spiral further, the race began.

The first 35 kilometers passed in a blur. I have little recollection of the thoughts that drifted in and out. But with about 7 kilometers to go, reality caught up with me. I began to feel the impact of injury and viral fever. My body began to revolt—stiffness, cramping, dizziness, a strange giddiness, like the floor beneath me might dissolve. The head spun. I felt on the edge of a blackout.

And then, I remembered those wise words that carried me through my first marathon, almost 10 years ago:

"If you can't fly, then run. If you can't run, then walk. If you can't walk, then crawl. But no matter what, keep moving forward."

So, I did.

Every time I noticed an empty stretch of road, I shut my eyes, not to escape, not to win, but just to endure. Each time I felt I might collapse, I found myself softly chanting, *"O Lord ... please carry me along."*

After what felt like an eternity, the finish line appeared. I crossed it. No fist pumps. No cheers. No celebration. Just a deep exhale. I folded my hands, closed my eyes, and whispered my gratitude to the skies for allowing me to try again.

Moments later, I looked at the watch. My heart skipped a beat.

3 hours, 02 minutes, 39 seconds.

Yes, it was a BQ. Again.

I had run the fastest marathon of my life, bettering my previous timing by a good seven minutes. I had comfortably qualified for Boston all over again, under surreptitiously spooky circumstances. Yes, I call them spooky for a reason. I had once chased this dream, every second, with desperation. I had obsessed, overtrained, overthought. Yet, I'd barely scraped through. But this time—after injury, undertrained, uncertain—I didn't chase time. I chased honesty. And somehow, that was enough. When you stop forcing the moment, the moment sometimes finds you.

Every full marathon taught me something, but none more so than my last full marathon at ATNDM 2025

The Comeback Curve–A.B.C.D Framework:

Over the years, I have had several ups and downs–a few ups and several downs, to be precise. Every time I toppled, I crawled my way back, painfully negotiating four phases. I call this the A.B.C.D of a typical comeback curve:

1. Acceptance; 2. Belief; 3. Clarity; 4. Discipline.

Stage ->	Acceptance	Belief	Clarity	Discipline
	...that something bad has happened.	**...that things will turn around eventually.**	**...on what actions will help turn things around.**	**...to relentlessly show up, day after day.**
Dos and Don'ts (for successful navigation)	• Don't indulge in self-pity or self-sympathy. Avoid getting into a "Why me?" rant. • Don't allow people to express sympathy for what happened–it's a massive waste of time. • Avoid the company of gossipmongers.	• Surround yourself with positive people, the ones who talk about hope and possibilities. • Visualize your happy, joyful, triumphant self.	• Keep it simple. • You don't need a long laundry list, just two or three simple, practical actions.	• Trust the process even if the results don't appear immediately. • Eliminate the option of not showing up.

Reflections from my comeback (after the back injury)	Following my back injury, it took me a while to accept that my hard-earned BQ, something that I had secured after years of hard work, had gone down the drain. But over time, I realized that fretting over the lost opportunity was not getting me anywhere. I also realized that I was a small, inconsequential cog in the bigger scheme of things. Things happen, not with the intent of hurting me or suiting me; they just happen. The moment that realization sank in, I found it easier to accept what had happened.	It's not that one fine day, I magically snapped out of the Mumbai debacle completely. Every now and then, the disturbing thought did come back. But I was fortunate to have friends who helped me build a positive frame of mind. With deliberate effort, I also learned the power of positive thinking, the power of joyful visualization. Just visualizing myself leaping into the air with a victorious fist pump was often enough to make me believe the possibility of great things ahead.	It took me a while to understand that resting is not the same as quitting. Sometimes, the best thing you can do to move forward is to take a pause. At some point, the clarity also sank in that for me to qualify for Boston again, I had to start running again, and for me to run again, I had to recover from the back injury. It was not rocket science, but simple, uncomplicated thinking. The moment I started thinking like that, the path ahead became clearer.	I have always been a big fan of the woodpecker. While searching for its food, it keeps hitting the tree bark, again and again, and again–till the bark yields! It's not that I didn't have my weak moments when my mind was playing all kinds of tricks, providing excuses to skip the planned run. But on each occasion, I chose to be the woodpecker. It's okay to fall, it's okay to feel miserable, it's okay to struggle ... but it's not okay to not show up. That's the mantra I always followed.

Yes, I had qualified again. And yes, I was expected to feel euphoric. But strangely enough, deep within, I didn't.

It was just a detail that was good to know. Nothing more. Nothing less. Just a detail.

The gift of feeling alive, all over again

In the weeks and months that followed, I kept running. I kept racing. And to my surprise, I kept getting faster. It felt like some unknown law of nature had taken over. The less I obsessed, the better I became.

I remembered the old Zen tale of the master pouring tea into an already full cup. That was me for years—a cup brimming with notions, expectations, pride, identity. Full of "me," so full that there was no space for grace.

But something shifted along the way. A quiet emptiness arrived. And with it, came surrender. With surrender came transformation.

They say there is divine power in a void, that the real magic happens in the realm of nothing. For a new painting to take shape, there has to be an empty canvas. My canvas was always too full, overcrowded with a medley of colors, leaving no space for new creation.

I always imagined myself to be the one who controlled things. It took me a lifetime to realize that countless events have had to happen the way they happened for me to be here, in this present moment. I couldn't have been the one orchestrating this unfathomably enormous sequence of events that led me up to the present moment. As a mediocre student of life, I never got that simple point. But then, nature has a way of nudging you along the path you are supposed to be on.

Acceptance is the final lap in every journey.

I have finally woken up to the reality. I was always being carried. Nudged. Guided. I had simply been too full of noise to notice.

Since that dark night in Mumbai, I've qualified for Boston twice. But I no longer feel about it the same way.

Something suddenly changed. Or maybe, it wasn't so sudden.

Something shifted the morning I couldn't run the NDM in 2018.

Something shifted during the 100 half marathons.

Something shifted the night my watch died during the 88th run when I cried.

Something shifted during that romantic 100-kilometer madness.

Something kept shifting, quietly, without my permission.

I hadn't noticed it. And now, the gradual shifts over time have aggregated to a bigger visible change, one that's difficult to ignore.

Throughout this book, I have talked about my dream of running the Boston Marathon. And if this were a linear story, it would ideally end with a triumphant finish of my maiden Boston Marathon at Boylston Street.

But now that I am here, I just don't feel about it the same way. I am not sure why these random thoughts keep me awake all night. I'm not sure I even want to run the Boston Marathon. And that thought scares me—it really scares me. Wasn't that the whole point, the so-called gold standard that I was chasing all this while?

I expectantly turn to "me" and "ME", the two troublemakers, to help me out. They have always been so loud all these years. But they conveniently choose to remain silent on this all-important question I am grappling with at this stage of my life. They offer no counsel, no argument. Just silence. So much for all the noise "they" have been creating all these years.

I keep turning the question over in my mind. Over and over. The more I think about it, the further I feel from the answer.

Maybe I never wanted to run in the Boston Marathon. Maybe I just needed a North Star, a distant dot on the horizon, to orient myself amidst all the chaos life so generously offers. And now, I fear what happens if I actually touch it. Where will I go from there?

That thought begins to clear the haze a little bit.

I don't want Boston to take centerstage. Not anymore. I want the spotlight to shine on something much deeper. I may have had a fleeting crush on the Boston Marathon. But it's the spirit of long-distance running that I fell madly in love with. That's what I want to celebrate.

Not the destination.

But the journey.

Not the pace.

But the perseverance.

Not the trophy.

But the truth.

The spirit of long-distance running that held me with both hands and got me back on my feet every time I toppled, that whispered to me in the dark, that taught me acceptance, that taught me the art of feeling alive, again and again. The sweet, sacred voice deep within, that always says:

"Just one more step, my friend…"

Just one more step, my friend!

Yes, I am a long-distance runner who has been running for over a decade now. How fast or slow I ran, where I ran or did not run, are finer details in the story, but they're not the story. The story itself is bigger, much bigger, than any of those footnotes.

That is true not just for me, but for every living person out there. It's not the finish line, but the fight. It's not the applause, but the silence. It's not the victory, but the will. Each one of us is a winner, not because we reached somewhere, but because we kept moving.

If someday, someone thinks of me, I don't want to be remembered as the guy who ran Boston. That so-called "gold standard" would be too trivial a detail to be remembered for. I'd rather be remembered as:

"Someone who never stopped trying. Never."

"Someone who lived the spirit of long-distance running every single day."

Key Messages

i. **Winning or losing may be context-dependent, but trying requires no context**. In life, we are all navigating our own unique context. Some may be more privileged than others, and some may have to combat bigger hardships than others. These contextual variations mean that we all have a different start line and finish line in the race of life. If that's the case, how can the end outcome alone be used as a benchmark to celebrate one's effort? It's the spirit of trying that matters.

ii. **Don't take yourself too seriously**. It took me years to appreciate that I am a small, inconsequential piece in the universe's unfathomably enormous jigsaw puzzle. I no longer feel the need to find patterns to explain why or how something happened. Instead, I am content with enjoying the roller-coaster ride with my loved ones, for as long as it lasts.

iii. **In the end, it doesn't even matter**. We are all creatures of desire. We spend a lifetime shaping and chasing our goals—goals that manifest in forms such as success, recognition, fame, appreciation, wealth, material possessions, sense of purpose, amongst several others. Sometimes, we get so hooked to these goals that the finer joys of life begin to fade. In the bigger scheme of things, these self-imposed goals don't even matter, certainly not as long as we have fun along the way and create memories worth reminiscing about.

AFTERWORD

The story concludes, but the journey doesn't.

GETTING into running was probably the best thing that ever happened to me.

Not because it made me faster or fitter, though it did; not because I ended up qualifying for the Boston Marathon, though I eventually did that too. But because it changed me at a level I didn't know I needed to change at. It rewired how I saw myself, moved through the world, and related to everything and everyone around me.

The story you've just read has a beginning and an end. But the journey it represents doesn't. In many ways, that journey has only just begun. Every run still teaches me something. Every day still asks me to show up. The struggles haven't disappeared, but I meet them differently now.

I am not the same man who started this journey. Somewhere along the way, something shifted. And the transformation didn't happen at the finish lines. It happened in the unnoticed, unglamorous moments—in the lonely early mornings, in moments of solitude, in setbacks, in the thousands of small choices I made without anyone noticing.

I became more aware of what really matters and more accepting of things that don't. The way I value time has changed. I no longer measure my days by how much I get done, but by how present I am. The way I deal with difficulty has changed. I still feel frustrated at times, but I'm less shaken by it. I don't expect things to be easy anymore, and I am able to gracefully accept it when things don't go my way. A quiet joy now runs through my life. I notice it when I wake up early and everything is still. I notice it after a long run, when the body is empty and the heart is full. I notice it in small, ordinary moments that I used to conveniently overlook.

And still, the biggest change I feel is something else: I feel more alive!

When I started running, I didn't expect it to change who I was. I was just trying to improve something on the surface. But somewhere along the way, I began to change from within. I was no longer chasing speed. I was trying to understand the person I had become.

Writing this book was never about celebrating a perfect ending. It was about tracing the mess, honoring the detours, and showing what it really looks like to change—not in one big leap, but in a thousand stumbles forward. If something in these pages spoke to you, then I am glad I wrote this book.

If you saw your own doubts, fears, and quiet courage in the book, I want you to know this: You're not alone.

And more important, you can do this too.

You don't need to be a runner. You don't need medals or podium finishes either. You just need to start. The rest will follow—not all at once, and not always in the way you expect, but it will.

So, wherever you are in your journey—starting, stumbling, restarting—I hope you carry this simple truth with you:

The race isn't against anyone else. It never was. It's just you versus you.

And that's the most meaningful race you'll ever run. You don't have to change everything. Just begin. You'll be surprised by how much is possible when you keep showing up.

Thank you for running a few miles with me. I hope to see you out there someday.

—Sundeep